My Viola and I

VIOLA :—" YES MY DEARS! AS A SOLOIST YOU HAVE ME TO RECKON WITH IN THE FUTURE!"

Cartoon by René Bull which appeared on the programme of a recital given by the author in the Wigmore Hall, London in 1911. The cellist should have been made to look much angrier than he does

LIONEL TERTIS

My Viola and I

A Complete Autobiography

With *Beauty of Tone in String Playing* and other essays

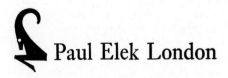 Paul Elek London

Published 1974 in Great Britain by
Elek Books Limited
54–58 Caledonian Road
London N1 9RN

ISBN 0 236 31040 2

Printed in Great Britain by
Ebenezer Baylis and Son Limited
The Trinity Press, Worcester, and London
Set in 11 pt. Ehrhardt, 1 pt. leaded

For my beloved wife
Lillian
without whom I could not
have compiled this book

Contents

viii *Contents*

For the String Player

Illustrations

Cartoon by René Bull, 1911 *(frontispiece)*

ix

Acknowledgments

I want to express first and foremost my deep gratitude to my dear friend Michael Kennedy, who most kindly offered to read the manuscript of this book. His corrections of some important factual mistakes are of most potent value to my autobiography. My grateful thanks also to my nephew Harold Milner who took charge of some of my papers in 1953 which would otherwise have been lost; to E.M.I. for their kind permission to reproduce the photograph of Solomon and I in the early 1930s, and that of myself taken by Angus McBean on the outside back cover of this book; and to Mr Erich Auerbach, the *Eastern Daily Press*, Mr Clive Barda, the *Radio Times* and other copyright-holders (see List of Illustrations) for their kind permission to reproduce copyright photographs in this book.

I should like to take the liberty of expressing, on behalf of all musicians and laymen alike, the great debt we owe to E.M.I. (H.M.V.) and other gramophone companies, for the wonderful way they continually improve their clever methods of eradicating the surface noises on old 78 records which once upon a time were accepted with equanimity; and particularly to Mr John Whittle, Manager of the Classical Department of E.M.I. Records, whose persistent efforts over the years, in this sphere, have enabled the modern public to hear the artists of bygone days. In my case I owe him a deep debt of gratitude for what he has done for the cause of the Viola – and is doing at the moment by issuing a new record to coincide with the publication of this autobiography.

I express my gratitude to Antony Wood of Paul Elek Ltd for his wonderful perceptiveness in editing my book and for his friendship – in spite of the work I have involved him in – which I shall ever treasure.

Author's Note

All royalties from the sale of this book are donated to the Musicians' Benevolent Fund, and I should like the reader to know a little about the activities of this magnificent organization, created over fifty years ago as a memorial to Gervase Elwes, the famous British tenor, who was killed at the age of fifty-five when he accidentally fell under a train in Boston, Mass.

The M.B.F. assists musicians in times of misfortune, illness, or when they are no longer able to carry on their professional activities. Since the time when its offices consisted of three rooms on the second floor of 16 John Street, London W.C.1, at a rental of £2 10s a week – where I first met the late Frank Thistleton, the then Secretary – the Fund has developed its work to a point at which its influence is far-reaching. No bona-fide claim from a professional musician is ever rejected. About 1,450 payments, by way of grants and pensions, were recently made in a single year to those who needed help. In addition to immediate grants of money and assistance with medical and surgical expenses the Fund maintains three Residential Homes and a Convalescent Home, from which musicians of all 'ranks' have benefited.

Foreword

What excuse is there for me to attempt to write an autobiography? It is this, that I grasp any and every opportunity, however incapable I may feel myself to be in literary accomplishments, to sing the praises again and again of what has been the love and tyrant of my life – the viola.

Bow and fiddle! The mind of man through the ages evolved these music-making instruments of such elegance, such resources, such power of expression, such endless possibilities, so enormously, tyrannically exacting, and at the same time so rewarding. Some of the scientifically minded of our time suggest that hand-made music is a passing phenomenon; they say that the music of the future will be something utterly different, produced in a mechanical laboratory and transmitted by means the radio has made familiar. Conductors, orchestras, soloists, concert rooms and conservatoires, according to these people, will be superseded, and looked upon as no less primitive than the Vikings who sailed their way from Norway to Labrador. I would have no wish to live, with these scientific friends, into that so-called 'brave new world'. It will have lost more than it will have gained. Be that as it may, as far as I am concerned (as I write in 1973 at the age of ninety-seven) no radio, no tape-recorder, no gramophone, however well they are manipulated, can compare with music performed in the flesh. The overcoming of difficulties, the struggle with the recalcitrant instrument, the wringing of beauty from contraptions of wood, hair, gut and metal – all this is something that makes life worth living. Music loses its vital personality when it is nothing more than a commodity obtained by turning a switch. Signs are already about us of that state of affairs. The music we value as the real thing *has* to be struggled for with all the power of the will, all possible concentration of the mind, struggled for, missed, and struggled for again. Those for whom background, superficial, senseless music (if we may refer to it as music) is a soothing noise, the jazz

band a help in conversation during a meal at a restaurant (ugh . . .
restaurant music – the means I call it of spoiling a good dinner),
have not the first notion of what music stands for.

My good fortune, I can see, is to have lived in an age when music
was in its heyday. In the England of my time the circle of the music-
loving increased decade by decade, greatly influenced by the
abundance of practical amateur musicians – so important to the
musical profession, and now, alas, fast disappearing, owing I would
say to the ease of turning a switch. Amateurs were more prolific in
the 1890s than in the 1880s and greater still after the turn of the
century. In mid-Victorian times we had lagged behind the continental countries. While I grew up the mass of Englishmen were dis-
covering music. We may be nearing the end of an epoch – the shades
of a mechanized world may be closing about us – but for the time
being it is still a wonderful age, an age when so far, thank goodness,
nobody has succeeded in inventing a mechanical fiddle and bow. I
would like to affirm that for me good music, during its enactment,
is by far the most absorbing and the most effective of the Arts in
bringing solace, comfort and *total* detachment from the worries of
the modern world.

There were two red-letter days for the viola, both of immense
significance to its cause as a solo instrument: one in 1779, when
Mozart created the Sinfonia Concertante for violin, viola and
orchestra, and the other in 1834 when Berlioz composed *Harold in
Italy* for orchestra and solo viola. Both these great men were conscious of the characteristic and attractive tone quality of the instrument. Mozart himself played the viola, and this particular work
contains some of his choicest music. The great violinist Paganini
also admired the timbre of the viola, and commissioned Berlioz to
write a work for it.

Before the advent of these two major works, the viola was un-
doubtedly the scullery-maid of the orchestra; indeed, Berlioz most
aptly described the viola as the 'Cinderella of the string family'. A
Cinderella, yes, but a Cinderella with a difference. The heroine of
the fairy tale was, as we all know, still quite young when her fortune
changed and she came into her rights, but it was not until the end of
the nineteenth century, and more particularly the twentieth century
– with the growing library of solo viola music, the fact that many
more violas of the right quality were becoming available and the
consequent ever-increasing number of skilled viola-players – that

the viola *really* began to consolidate its position as a solo instrument and earn still further its right to a place in the sun.

Of necessity this autobiography includes a good deal that was contained in a short memoir I started to write off the cuff in 1945 entitled *Cinderella No More*, which was published in 1953 by Peter Nevill and has been out of print since about 1955. In the present book I have considerably filled out in both substance and detail the account of my life up to the end of the Second World War there given, and of course I have a good deal to say of my life since then. In addition, I include, in a separate part of the book, an extensively revised and expanded version of my treatise *Beauty of Tone in String Playing*, which was first published by Oxford University Press in 1938 and twice reprinted before going out of print in the early 1950s; an essay *The Art of String Quartet Playing*, based in part on a short article I wrote for my friend Richard Capell in 1947 entitled *The String Quartet*; a paper I read on 2 December 1954 at a meeting of the Composers' Concourse held in London; and the lecture I gave at the Wigmore Hall on 4 December 1950 at a demonstration of the Tertis Model viola. I have also compiled a list of violinmakers in seventeen countries who make the Tertis Model viola, and a selection of works published and unpublished for viola solo with which I have been concerned. Finally, Malcolm Walker, Editor of *The Gramophone*, has kindly compiled a discography of my recordings in as much detail as may be ascertained.

Any shortcomings from the literary point of view in this book, I ask the reader to forgive. They are entirely due to my lack of scholastic tuition.

L.T.

My Viola and I

I

Formative Years

My first rather vague recollection of childhood is of being hoisted up on to a chair for my hands to be placed on the keys of the antediluvian upright family piano which was never used. But my memory is very definite of my howls of delight when my fumbling fingers drew forth sounds from the instrument. As soon as I became aware that I was an entity I began to realize that at times I laughed but mostly I think I cried. My mother had found the antidote for my excessive crying. The result of this first musical excitement, however, was that my craving to get at the piano became the bane of my mother's existence. I wanted to strum at every possible opportunity.

My father, Alexander Tertis, was born at Koudanov in the Russian province of Minsk, and arrived in London at the age of thirteen, eventually becoming a naturalized Briton. My mother, who was a veritable angel, was Polish born and was brought to England as a child by her father who also became a British subject. I am therefore British and very proud of it.

My birth certificate states that I was born at 14 Regent's Place, West Hartlepool in the County of Durham on 29 December 1876. I cannot say with Thomas Hood 'I remember, I remember the house where I was born', for I left my birthplace for London when I was but three months old. Thirty-four years elapsed before I returned there to take part in a concert as solo violist with Melba; we arrived in a fog and left in a fog, and that is all I know of my native town.

My father was a Jewish minister, and his singing at the synagogue attracted worshippers from near and far. My evident inclination for music was also stirred by his practising at home. He had a fine tenor voice, and later on I began to realize how beautiful his phrasing was – he was naturally musical, good music absorbed him, and to him principally I owe my passion for it.

3

My parents must have been impressed by my persistent demon-strative eagerness to get to the piano when I was about three years old, for they called in a strange, funny-looking old man, who thence-forth came frequently to show my tiny fingers how to play. The eventual result of his regular teaching was that I made my first public appearance on the concert platform at six years of age. I well recall my self-possession and total lack of nervousness when I made my first bow to an audience. I can remember as if it were yesterday that I was dressed for the occasion in a black velvet coat and deep white lace collar. I played a Tarantella by Stephen Heller, and did so at a most excessive pace to show off! My teacher, who rejoiced in the name of Wasserzug (which means 'water-train'), proud of my first venture in public, said to me after the performance, 'We will play a duet together at a concert and you will have the treble part.' The next day being my piano lesson, he took me meticulously through what I had to perform, giving me directions exactly how to practise it. When I had learnt it sufficiently well he joined me in a rehearsal. As we proceeded he suddenly stopped me at a bar in which his right hand was in very close proximity to my left hand. The passage was marked forte and he complained that my little finger was not nearly loud enough, so we went back a few measures, and when we arrived at the bar of complaint I resolved to do my best to please him. Lifting my hand high, I brought it down with *all* the strength of which I was capable, to give *all* the emphasis I could to the note complained of. The sound that came from this effort was not a musical one; instead there was a fearful howl from my teacher – my finger nail had dug into his little finger and drawn blood!

Needless to say, the duet with old 'Water-train' never took place either in public or in private. However, in spite of this unfortunate episode he still went on teaching me for five or six years. I remember distinctly that he always held his umbrella (never a stick) in his fist under the pit of his arm with the point sticking out high up behind his back most dangerously. One day when I was out walking with him I had the temerity to say to him: 'You shouldn't carry your umbrella like that – you will poke somebody's eye out!'

Although I was complimented on my technical facility I never liked the piano. As a consequence I was not diligent and my mother came to the point of locking me in the room with it. There I 'prac-tised' for many hours a day running my fingers over the keys, frivo-lously playing scales, etc. while most of the time I had a story book in front of me instead of the music! Such was my wickedness when I was barely seven years old.

Some of my earliest memories are of the east end of London. We lived at 8 Princelet Street, Spitalfields – 'spital' being a corruption of 'hospital' – a Victorian slum in the borough of Stepney. In an adjacent street which bore the name of Brick Lane, the 'poor man's market' was held every Sunday morning. It presented a scene I still remember, with its piles of cast-off clothing and second-hand boots and shoes spread out on the ground for sale, to say nothing of the din and babble of excited bargaining crowds.

Nearby, across a main road about five minutes from my home, was Petticoat Lane. This thoroughfare was a place of such intensity of squalor that I wonder I have lived to tell my tale. Situated at the end of it was a Board School in which I spent my childhood days. The educational curriculum at this institution was to say the least of it sparse and haphazard. I seem to remember that compulsory education, such as it was at that time, had been instituted only six years before I was born – costing parents threepence a week.

I also vividly recall how, during the break for recreation, we children raced out into the street to reach a man with a wheelbarrow upon which he carried a glowing brazier for frying potato chips. I generally succeeded in being first to get to him when I would purchase a pennyworth. He would put a generous helping straight into a piece of old newspaper torn from a pile that he had on his barrow, and to add to the delicacy would anoint them with a liberal sprinkling from a bottle of vinegar. We would stroll up and down the street thoroughly enjoying this sumptuous repast – it included no doubt some of the print which must have come off the vinegar-soaked newspaper, but I do not remember that any ill effects resulted.

At the tender age of eight I could not imagine that some dozen years later the potato in another form would turn out to be a valuable asset to my efforts for the shunned viola. Towards the end of the 1890s, when I first began playing solos whenever an opportunity offered, whether for a few shekels or for nothing at all, it was the baked potato, not the fried one, which came to my assistance. Artists' rooms in those days, if such they could be called, had no vestige of warmth, nor hot water, let alone any other convenience! I recollect that London street corners at that time were often occupied by barrows similar to the fried potato one of my schooldays, the

owners of which cried out: 'All 'ot, all 'ot, baked taters!' In winter
time I never failed, as a preliminary to my playing, to fondle grate-
fully the hot homely vegetable which reposed in each of my overcoat
pockets, so that I had a semblance of warm fingers before going
into action.

The one bright spot in Spitalfields for me was Christchurch, so
tall, so elegant, so graceful, with its lovely pale grey stone. Our
house in Spitalfields was early Victorian, big, antiquated and
rambling. The kitchen and scullery were basement dungeons into
which only a modicum of light penetrated through windows each
of which faced a shallow bricked-up sunken area. In close proximity
was a wooden stable where my father kept the pony which drew the
trap he used for visiting the members of his parish. One day the
unfortunate animal's back legs slipped down into one of the sunken
areas and I remember my father and uncle grasping his hind-
quarters and hoisting him up to safety. The pony, a docile creature,
didn't seem to resent this treatment in the slightest and suffered
no injury.

As a young boy I attended the services at the synagogue across the
road from our house. I understood hardly a word of Hebrew. Well
I remember how hypocritical I felt myself to be, pretending to
supplicate the Supreme Being in words I did not comprehend, and
for this reason, whenever I possibly could I surreptitiously avoided
attending the House of Worship.

Never did the idea of the piano becoming my principal instrument appeal to me. I felt even in those early days that its response to
one's expressive effort was inadequate, and I have always considered
the piano, for this reason, a far more difficult music-making instrument than the fiddle. Pianists abound, but how few and far between
are those who can make a melodic phrase on that instrument warmly
expressive – as a string player is much more easily able to do
through the employment of circumspect vibrato. All through my
study of the piano my ambition was to become a violinist. When I
was twelve years of age I realized that to achieve this it would be
necessary to utilize my piano playing professionally to acquire the
wherewithal for violin lessons. My parents, both of whom had gentle
and generous dispositions, encouraged my musical aspirations as
best they could, but they were not affluent and it was further borne
in upon me that I must do something to relieve the family budget
as well as to satisfy my longing to play a string instrument. Another

influence was my desire to get away from the dreary, squalid neigh-bourhood of Spitalfields.

At the age of thirteen therefore, with my parents' permission I left home to earn my living. They knew I was very confident for my age and well able to look after myself, and this decided them to allow me to leave home. As an illustration of their trust in my capabilities – at the age of twelve I took my mother, younger brother and sister (whose ages were eight and nine) to Brighton for the day, bought the excursion tickets and organized the day's activities which included the taking of a photograph by a beach photographer on Brighton promenade, the cost of which was sixpence. I arranged the grouping of the picture as I wanted it and I remember my mother looking charming in a bonnet tied with ribbon under her chin. It is always a source of regret to me that I should have lost this photograph.

Another adventure in which I was involved occurred very soon after this. My father, with his pony and trap, was visiting his parishioners in Bayswater when the shaft of the trap and harness broke and he had to leave them to be repaired. Poor father had ignominiously to walk the pony home. When the shaft and harness were put right he was too busy to fetch them, and I was deputed to do so. I rode the pony bareback from Spitalfields, through the City and Oxford Street to Bayswater, and subsequently drove both pony and trap quite safely home. Oxford Street in 1889 was thronged with horse traffic and I distinctly recall that I felt quite important with my achievement.

Before leaving home to earn my living I consulted two musical papers, *The Era* and *The Stage*, both of which carried numerous advertisements for instrumentalists. My first engagement was as a member of a so-called Hungarian band. At that time Hungarian bands were distinctly in fashion. We wore uniforms which made us look more like brigands than Hungarians; we were in fact all British! My collaboration with this not particularly inspiring team was for a summer season in various seaside resorts. Many other short-time jobs came my way – I tumbled out of one into another. A position I remember vividly was that of accompanist to a blind street musician in Brighton. He was an excellent violinist and a lovable man. I lodged at his apartments and every morning his attendant arrived with a bijou piano upon a barrow. The three of us went forth and on the promenade where Brighton joins Hove, the violinist gave excellent performances of music by Vieuxtemps,

Wieniawski and composers of similar category. Our attendant with money-box in hand solicited contributions from a usually large audience who were attracted by the violinist's playing, and the takings were good. For my share as pianist and accompanist I was given a generous weekly salary.

At the termination of my engagement with the blind man, in the summer of 1892 I obtained an eleven-week contract with a small group of instrumentalists who were performing on the pier at Southend-on-Sea. The sort of pay I earned compared with the standards of today was exceedingly meagre, but by practising economy I managed to add to my savings. In fact, I now had sufficient funds to enter Trinity College of Music, London, as a student. I was nearly sixteen.

To peer back in memory to the London of those days is like looking at another world, one I am sure, unless memory deceives me, of a more vivacious, sanguine and carefree race of Britons than that of today. Without motor horns and the infliction of roaring aircraft, it was considerably less noisy. It is certainly no illusion to say that the clatter of horse-drawn vehicles was more bearable than latter-day noises; the typical London sound – the tinkling of the bells of hansom cabs – was delicate and merry. Affluence was not mine, but in those days pence had a real purchasing power. Oranges were three or four for a penny, and the omnibus fare from Liverpool Street to Piccadilly was 'tuppence'. An omnibus was drawn by two horses and was more like an Irish jaunting car but much taller, with the driver sitting in front and often conversing with the passengers seated side by side. At Southend my pay had been two pounds a week, and on this I not only lived but saved. (Be it said that I never indulged in the expense of meat during my sojourn there.)

Between the time of leaving home and 1892 I had become the possessor of a violin of sorts and been given a few spasmodic lessons from a man who I afterwards realized must have been the world's worst violin teacher. His name was Fenigstein, and he could well have ruined me as a string player. He had cultivated a left-hand technique of breath-taking rapidity. Scales of fingered octaves, all of which were interspersed with many diminished and augmented ones, were taken at lightning speed in an appallingly slip-shod manner. What wickednesses were his! Faulty intonation was never corrected, the accuracy of note values never insisted upon; he cared nothing about how the bow and fiddle were held. This brings me to the first essential for the embryo string player – to have a thoroughly good teacher, one possessing musicianship and well capable of *demonstrating* the multitudinous technicalities of violin playing. How can a poor executant be a good teacher? The notion that he might possibly be able to teach what he cannot perform is a dangerous paradox, one that I would denounce without mercy. The teacher is a menace who cannot demonstrate his art at a pitch that will arouse the pupil's ambitions and enthusiasm. The embryo fiddler must be naturally musical, must begin very young, and must have time for application. Nor is this enough: he should frequently and habitually listen to the greatest virtuosi; there is no more potent incentive. With the savings accrued from my professional engagements as a pianist I was able to attend a few concerts given by famous artists before entering Trinity College of Music.

2

Student Days

Well do I recall my excitement at the thought of entering Trinity College in the never-to-be-forgotten Michaelmas term of 1892. My principal study was the piano, with R. W. Lewis, an excellent teacher and pianist. My second study was the violin with B. M. Carrodus who was well known as a performer and again an excellent pedagogue. As for my harmony lessons with Dr Saunders, I confess I have not the smallest recollection of him, having no particular interest in the rudiments of that subject at the time. But the College, in its archives, has me down as having been in his class.

I made considerable progress with the piano, playing concertos with the College orchestra, and I also had a few lessons on the organ during my short stay. But my prevailing concern and pleasure were my violin lessons. My savings saw me through only two terms, ending with the Lent term of 1893, and then I had to go out into the world once more to earn the wherewithal for further tuition. Whenever this state of the exchequer became apparent, I would immediately resort to a copy of *The Era*, which was devoted mainly to theatrical and music-hall interests, and was usually crammed with advertisements offering vacancies for all sorts of instrumentalists – especially pianists. Invariably it was not long before I secured an engagement.

A lucrative offer which immediately presented itself was for a musician-attendant at a lunatic asylum at Preston in Lancashire. I distinctly remember I had no qualms in being prepared to undertake this, and with the aid of a recommendation from Professor Bradbury-Turner, the then Principal of Trinity College, I obtained the post. I will quote the letter he was good enough to address to me shortly after I arrived at Preston, because of the deep impression it made upon me – it helped me throughout the course of my life – and because of its Victorian flavour.

I am glad to hear you have got the appointment, and I trust you will be able to push on with your studies. You are very young, and it is a pity you are taken away so early from the necessary course, but we have to do the best for ourselves under such conditions. Many of our very best men have had to labour under the same difficulties, and have succeeded and been all the better for it. As I said, you are young and just the age for work and to achieve anything. Let me hope nothing will be allowed to draw you away from the right path and, as Schumann says in his maxims: 'The laws of morality are also the laws of Art.' I trust you will have a good future. Remember – Study is unending.

Signed: Bradbury-Turner

My duties at the asylum, together with other musician-attendants, included – besides making music – what one might call domestic chores, such as assisting the patients to dress themselves, and helping them to behave as far as their mental capacity would allow. I remember our playing seemed to awaken in them some sort of interest, but their mental condition so terribly destitute of any expectation saddened me, and the hopelessness of the general atmosphere in the institution was more than I could endure for long and forced me to look for another source of income. The head of the little band of musician-attendants was an excellent oboe-player with whom I got on very well. I have always loved the timbre of the oboe when well played and he was an admirable executant. He tried to teach me this fascinating instrument in our spare time, but he soon gave up the attempt – I was a dismal failure.

From the asylum, again via *The Era*, I was soon engaged at Clacton-on-Sea as pianist at an establishment which rejoiced in the name of 'Rigg's Retreat'. It was owned by an amateur violinist named Badger who catered mainly for East London school treats. My main occupation was accompanying him on the piano in his violin-playing to hundreds of children in an enormous dining hall during their meals. Badger, a tolerable and enthusiastic violinist, was an extraordinarily corpulent man, and there remains in my mind a ludicrous preliminary to our performances. He was obliged to loosen and readjust his braces, for only in this way, so he explained, could he reach the G string with his bow with any degree of comfort! At the end of the tea-time meal when the clatter of cups and saucers had practically subsided, he stood up, announced to the children that he would play them a solo and asked for complete silence. He thereupon invariably indulged in what is commonly known as 'sob stuff', adding his own sentimentality to the full until I positively squirmed on my music stool. I was always glad when this ordeal was over. However, there was one thing I had to thank him for; he gave me a most useful tip when one had little time to practise, which was that one's fingers could be kept supple by closing the fist very tightly and then violently and stiffly throwing out the fingers to their full extent, the exercise being performed several times a day.

With my funds replenished from these and other engagements, I was able to return to Trinity College for a further term of three months. This time, to my satisfaction, I concentrated on violin lessons only with B. M. Carrodus. As a result of this period of intensified work on the instrument of my choice I was fired with the ambition to go abroad for further tuition. It was being continually impressed upon me that continental musical training, particularly string playing, was far better than our own – a fallacious supposition I was soon to discover, and one with which I eventually most vehemently disagreed. So far as the violin was concerned, there were teachers in London second to none, such as Arbos and Rivarde at the Royal College of Music, Emile Sauret and Willy Hess at the Royal Academy of Music. All these players were virtuosi, and watching them and hearing them I found to be a great incentive to my ambitions.

However, I had heard so much of the great traditions of the Leipzig Conservatorium that I resolved to go there by hook or by crook. There was a superstitious reverence for Leipzig in the England of that time, thanks to Mendelssohn, to whom the reputation of the Conservatorium was due, even though he had been dead for more than forty years. How greatly this famous school of music had deteriorated I was soon to find out.

With my mother's help, through her sparse savings, I was able to realize my desire and get to Leipzig in proud possession of a new passport, which in those days consisted of a single foolscap sheet with the following words: 'WE, John Earl of Kimberley – Peer of the United Kingdom – Knight of the Most Noble Order of the Garter – request and require in the name of Her Majesty – to allow Lionel Tertis travelling on the Continent – to pass freely without let or hindrance – '.

I managed to stay in Leipzig for a six-month course. The cele-brated Gewandhaus orchestral concerts provided fuel for my musical passion and were the only real benefit I got (the conductor at that time was the famous Arthur Nikisch). I learnt precious little from my teachers and particularly little in my principal study, the violin. My tutor, Professor Bolland, paid small or no attention to what or how I played. His room at the Conservatorium was an extremely long one, I played at one end, and during most of my lesson he was generally at the other extremity of it engrossed in his collection of postage stamps! English and American students were there in numbers in my time, and no love was lost between us and the German students. Feelings were expressed not in mere casual blows but in pitched battles. The authorities well knew of this but never troubled to interfere.

I lodged in the house of an English family – a gross mistake on my part for I learnt little of the German language. However, I dis-covered that by using it in my own ungrammatical way I could always make myself understood. I became good friends with a German of about my own age, a furrier by trade who had a shop in Leipzig, was fond of music and liked the sounds I produced from my violin. Together we took long walks, and during the course of one of them we came across a junk shop which had a string instru-ment displayed in the window. I found it to be an attractive-looking viola with an unusually pale varnish and labelled 'Albani'. I had never thought of playing the viola, but I considered the instrument such a fine specimen of craftsmanship that I longed to have it, though the price asked, about £25, was beyond my meagre resources.

My desire to own the instrument so impressed my furrier friend that he insisted on lending me the money to buy it. When I returned to England I took my prize home and it lay in its case for a consider-able time without bridge, soundpost or strings. Eventually I met a keen amateur viola-player, a Mr Salt of Shrewsbury, who appealed to me and I let him have it for what I had paid for it. Never for one moment did it come into my mind that one day I should become fanatically devoted to the beautiful tone quality of the viola. I was only just getting to know a little bit about the violin, in which all my interests were centred. (My dealings with the first viola I ever owned had an astonishing sequel more than sixty years later. At a morning rehearsal which I attended as a listener at the Royal Festival

Hall, I believe it was the L.P.O. but I am not positive, a member of the viola section showed me the instrument he was playing; to my astonishment, it was the same Albani I had purchased in Leipzig which he had bought from Mr Salt! Of course I had acquired this lovely instrument at a time when the 'Cinderella of the string family' could be obtained at a very nominal sum. I imagine the value of this instrument today is at least twenty or thirty times the price I paid for it.)

After six months' sojourn in Leipzig I came back to London towards the end of 1895 and became an intermittent student at the Royal Academy of Music. The Academy at that time was not housed in its present spacious building in Marylebone Road. Its original home was in a number of ill-adapted old houses in Tenterden Street off Hanover Square – a rabbit-warren consisting of mostly small rooms connected by creaking, antediluvian short staircases. On each little landing one would find a music room large enough to house a piano. But the building also boasted a meagre-sized concert hall.

My first term was paid for by Lionel de Rothschild. Young, hard-up and ambitious as I was, and on the strength of my having the same Christian name, I had written to him to state my case, having heard of his generosity to others. The reply was to the effect that Mr de Rothschild would like a note from the Principal of the Academy, Sir Alexander Mackenzie, concerning my capabilities. I played to Sir Alexander – himself a violinist – and the result was a ten-pound note from Rothschild. So it came about, together with help from various engagements I undertook, that I studied the violin at the Academy, on and off, under Hans Wessely until the end of 1897.

One outside job I remember during my studentship was as leader of a quintet, or perhaps it was a sextet, at Madame Tussaud's, dressed in a peculiar garb of archaic military cut. As the leader I used to play compositions replete with sentimentality in every programme, and I recollect Wessely coming one day to hear what I was doing and I happened to be playing a charming piece of Victorian flavour called *Andante Religioso* by Thomé! These concerts were held every afternoon, but it was all grist to the mill and provided me with funds for further tuition.

From the age of thirteen I had lived like a wandering Arab, but I eventually found a habitation which proved to be a more permanent lodging. At the Academy I made friends with a fellow violin student, Spencer Dyke, who came from Plymouth and we shared an apartment in Greencroft Gardens, Hampstead. We were both full of ambition, and would vie with each other in the amount of practice we accomplished during the day. We spent our holidays together, seeking out some quiet seaside village where we could work undisturbed. One summer we found ourselves at Corton near Great Yarmouth, and the holiday stays in my mind because Dyke was furiously practising Bach's Chaconne from the Partita No. 2 in D minor at the time. When he had a difficulty to overcome, he would stand in a corner of the room facing the wall, slaving away and permitting nothing to distract him for unconscionable periods. He always said that was the position in which he could exercise most concentration.

Professor Wessely was a good fiddler, a classical player, rather cold, but possessed a fine technical ability. He was dictatorial, inclined to be conceited, and as a teacher rather harsh. He taught well up to a point – only up to a point, however, for the most important tricks of the trade he jealously kept to himself. He was an able quartet leader, and I learnt much from him about chamber-music playing later on, when I was the violist in his quartet. I once witnessed a strange incident brought on by acute nervousness – all the more unaccountable since the self-assured Wessely was usually the master of his nerves. He was playing Saint-Saëns's sparkling Introduction and Rondo Capriccioso at one of our quartet concerts, and at the place in the work where a long glissando chromatic scale occurs from the top of the fiddle, his bow got on the wrong side of the bridge. There it danced for the whole length of the glissando down the E string. We heard a long succession of squeaks before he realized what he was doing and jumped the bow back to its rightful position.

In my early stages at the Academy Wessely, who was Viennese, thought poorly of my efforts, and he told my father – though I heard nothing of this until much later – that I had better give up the violin, being more fitted for the grocery trade! However my father resented this and my lessons continued. When I reached the age of nineteen a fellow violin student, Percy Hilder Miles, came to me with the suggestion that I should take up the viola. He wanted to form a string quartet, and there was not one viola student at the Academy! So casual was my discovery of my mission in life, of that beautiful, soon-to-be-beloved viola, to which I was to devote the rest of my days.

The idea of playing in a string quartet excited me. I borrowed an instrument from the Academy, and was immediately interested in its attractive quality of tone, so distinct from the other members of the string family though it was as usual a small viola, incapable of true C string sonority. I worked at it for a week, mastering the clef, and the quartet then met. We rehearsed an early Beethoven work for about a fortnight, and it was then arranged that we should play to the Principal. I can see the old Tenterden Street concert hall now, with Mackenzie sitting alone in the auditorium listening to us. Afterwards he came to the platform and asked me how long I had been playing the viola. When I said three weeks, his reply was, 'Well, in my opinion you will never regret it.'

Thenceforward I worked hard and, being dissatisfied with my teacher – who was a violinist and knew little of the idiosyncrasies of the viola, nor indeed was there any pedagogue worthy of the name to go to for guidance – I resolved to continue my study by myself. I consider that I learnt to play principally through listening to virtuosi; I lost no opportunity of attending concerts to hear great artists perform. I especially remember hearing Sarasate at the old St James's Hall playing the Mendelssohn concerto most marvellously – every note a pearl.

When I first began to play the viola as a solo instrument, prejudice and storms of abuse were my lot. The consensus of opinion then was that the viola had no right to be heard in solos, indeed the consideration of its place in the string family was of the scantiest. It was not only a despised instrument, but its cause was far from helped by the down-and-out violinists who usually played it. The executants in those days were violinists too inferior to gain a position in orchestras as such. A wretchedly low standard of viola-playing was in fact accepted simply and solely because there was no alternative. A little old man, said to be a professional viola-player, was engaged by the Academy to take part twice a week in the orchestral practices. What a player he was! He used a very small instrument, not worthy of the name viola, and he produced from it as ugly a sound as fiddle ever emitted – a bone-dry tone, absolutely devoid of vibrato, which made one's hair stand on end. I once enquired of Sir Alexander: 'Could we not dispense with this horrible player?' His reply was, 'No, he is a necessary evil.'

Mackenzie, in addition to his violinistic talent, gained as a composer a position alongside Sullivan, Parry and Stanford as one of the leaders of the British musical renaissance. It was his destiny in the latter part of his life to eclipse his creative reputation by the extraordinary ability he showed as a teacher and administrator. The Academy, when he became its Principal in 1888, was in low water. The general inefficiency of the institution had led to the founding of the Royal College of Music, which with Grove, Parry and Stanford as its leading spirits was soon to grow from strength to strength. Mackenzie's glory is to have restored the Academy to prosperity and a brilliant position in the pedagogical history of music in England despite the powerful competition in South Kensington. Mackenzie was a man of strong personality, a linguist and a wit. His drawback was his temper. He could be ungovernably violent. I remember how a talented boy, still in knickerbockers, turned up one day with his first orchestral work. There were some mistakes in the manuscript, and Mackenzie, who conducted the twice-a-week orchestral practices, exploded with wrath at the faults in the score, going for the boy so furiously before the orchestra that the poor little composer went away in tears, vowing he would never write another note. His name was York Bowen. Happily he did not carry out his threat, but wrote many more notes, including a symphony, three piano concertos, a violin concerto, a viola concerto, a viola sonata and a quartet for four violas, besides numerous piano works. He was himself a most efficient pianist and could play both viola and horn.

Mackenzie's compositions are hardly ever heard nowadays, and no doubt many of them are dead beyond recall, including his series of festival cantatas, settings of wishy-washy texts which he, clever man that he was, could never have really believed in. There are many other creations of his of major stature and I recall with pleasure some of his instrumental works, the Pibroch for violin and orchestra, for instance, and a brilliant piano quartet. Sarasate used to play the Pibroch and the violin concerto, works one would have thought worthy of revival at the Edinburgh Festival, for Mackenzie was an Edinburgh man. But his centenary passed unnoticed at Edinburgh in 1947.

In 1897 a fellow student lent me a Guadagnini viola. It had, alas, been cut down in size as usual, but the tone was far better than that of the Academy instrument, and from that moment I became more than ever an enthusiast, resolved that my life's work should

3

be the establishment of the viola's rights as a solo instrument.

In those days when it was the rarest thing to hear a viola solo, the upper range of the instrument was completely unexplored. Players of that time rarely climbed higher than the second leger line in the treble clef! To counteract this neglect of the higher registers I resolved to give demonstrations to show the improvement in the quality of those higher tones that could be achieved by persistent practice in them. As a student at the R.A.M. I was able to accomplish this by playing the Mendelssohn and Wieniawski D minor concertos (of course a fifth lower but exactly as written for the violin) at two of the fortnightly students' concerts there. The morning after my performance of the Mendelssohn, I met Alfred Gibson who was for a time the violist of the Joachim Quartet. Evidently he had been present at the concert for he greeted me with a menacing look and exploded: 'I suppose the next thing is, you will be playing behind the bridge! The viola is not meant to be played high up – that is the pig department!' I felt like replying: 'It probably is on *your* viola but not on mine!' However, that would have been rude coming from a student to a Professor of the Academy.

After leaving the R.A.M. to earn my living, I returned there for a while in 1899–1900, when I was appointed sub-professor of the viola. One of my duties was to play in the weekly string ensemble class conducted by that great violinist and pedagogue Emile Sauret, then professor of the violin at the R.A.M. He possessed the most amazing left-hand technique, and his bow arm too was wonderful – in fact he was a virtuoso in the true sense of the word. He turned out a galaxy of brilliant fiddlers during his professorship. He was a delightful jolly Frenchman, whose English, in spite of all the years he spent in London, remained sketchy. The long, tedious journey to Vienna by boat and train once drew from him the remark: 'Tank God we are arrive!' But he could be witty. I remember one occasion during the string ensemble class. The leader turned up with a violin varnished in a most startling red colour. Directly Sauret perceived it he put down his baton and bawled at the leader: 'From where have you get that Whitechapel lobster!'

3

Back Desk to Front Desk

In 1901 I was appointed full professor of the viola and my playing must have improved for Hans Wessely invited me to become a member of the Wessely String Quartet. I accepted, and after a number of rehearsals, my first professional engagement with the quartet was at the Holloway Polytechnic, London, for which I received the handsome fee of five shillings.

After finally leaving the Royal Academy of Music as a student, I obtained a position as violinist in Henry Wood's Queen's Hall orchestra. I was the last player at the last desk of the second violins. Arthur Payne, a well-known and excellent violinist, led the orchestra in those days.

I worked at the viola in my spare hours. Henry Wood got to know of this and asked to hear me play with the result that I jumped from last violinist to principal viola in the orchestra. Meanwhile I continued in a number of concerts with the Wessely Quartet, and one day Wessely produced a copy of a work by Mozart entitled *Sinfonia Concertante*, for violin, viola and orchestra. We went through it together and were enchanted. Where he got it from I do not remember – possibly on one of his frequent visits to Vienna, for he was in his early days a pupil of Professor Grün at the Conservatoire there. Eventually we performed it in public at the Queen's Hall with Henry Wood conducting. I think I am right in saying it was the first performance in London (although Hallé had already conducted two performances in Manchester, in 1868 and 1873, I have recently discovered). Very little notice was taken of it, indeed I can remember that one paper referred to it as a 'five finger exercise'! – a rather surprising comment for a work containing some of Mozart's choicest music.

It was during these early activities of mine that I began to hear glowing accounts of the violinist Fritz Kreisler who was just appearing on the horizon. For me the experience of hearing him was like falling in love. His glowing tone, his vibrato, unique and inexpressively beautiful, his phrasing which in everything he played was so wonderful and so peculiarly his own, his extraordinarily fine bowing and left-hand technique, his attitude at once highly strung and assured, the passionate sincerity of his interpretations – all this made me follow him around like a dog wherever he played in this country.

My mind recalls again and again the tremendous impression on me of his first appearance in 1901 when I heard him give a breathtaking and unmatchable performance of the Brahms violin concerto. I was thrilled to the marrow – such matchless string playing from every point of view was the nearest thing to perfection that I think mortal man could experience. At the end of one of his recitals which he gave at the Crystal Palace I could not help running after him. He was leaving with a mutual friend Pedro Morales, a Spanish poet and composer who studied music in Seville and at the Royal College of Music; Morales remained in London most of his life. Overcome by the effect of Kreisler's marvellous playing I blurted out to him: 'Mr Kreisler, would you give me some lessons?' To which he replied: 'What do you want lessons for? Besides, my dear friend, I travel so much I have no time.' The most unbelievable of all unbelievable happenings to me that day would have been that a time would come when I was to enjoy the great privilege, honour and delight of playing with Kreisler – in New York, Boston, Mass. and London – Mozart's Sinfonia Concertante for violin and viola. The crowning experience of my life has been to rehearse and perform in public with this prince of men.

I remember in the 'prehistoric' days of gramophone recording hearing on a cylindrical Edison record a lovely melody that Kreisler had played into it. It was not published and I recollect taking it down bit by bit, a laborious process which involved many hours of really concentrated listening. Eventually I produced this melody as an 'Air on the G string' which I have to this day in manuscript. Ultimately Kreisler's playing of it into this Edison contraption was published and turned out to be entitled *Sarabande* by Sulzer. My version was in a different key with variations in the piano part and slight alterations here and there in the solo part.

From the very early days of gramophone record manufacture, I made scores and scores of 78 records for solo viola for two companies. One of these, for which I began recording in 1920, was the

Aeolian-Vocalian company. This was one of the first companies to attempt the manufacture of long-playing records, but I am sorry to say that their efforts, although they made hundreds of records, were a dismal failure. The scratching hiss on them was unbelievably appalling and the result of their valiant attempts eventually brought about their bankruptcy. My dear colleague the late Albert Sammons and I made innumerable records for them, and what became of them I do not know, but I managed to save a few as curiosities.

But the principal company for which I made records was Columbia. When one thinks back to the inception of gramophone recording one wonders how we could have put up with the awful drawbacks of 1) having to limit each record to exactly four minutes and 2) the continuous scratchy noise in the background. For example, in the Mozart Sinfonia Concertante for violin, viola and orchestra one had to break into the music every four minutes, with the result that the work was interrupted no fewer than eight times, i.e. four double-sided records. It is astonishing to think now how we could have accepted this extraordinary travesty of music translation and tolerated such iniquities with such astounding equanimity. But even this was progress compared with the very first time I attempted to make a wax record, which must have been at the end of the nineteenth century. I have a vague memory of playing into an antediluvian coaching horn, and when I wanted to play softly or loudly, having to step backwards or forwards towards the horn while actually performing. (At the end of this book will be found details of some of these records that I made – but there must have been many more.)

Another example of our ready acceptance of extremely disagreeable conditions in those days was the fact that underground trains at the beginning of the 1890s were hauled by steam engines. Baker Street in particular was a station I alighted at or departed from very frequently. The smoke from the engines poured continually through the tunnels at both ends of the platform, and we were obliged to inhale it while waiting for the train to appear. But at that time such an everyday 'nicety' was looked upon as just another 'necessary evil' – though I suppose this kind of thing was as nothing really compared to the pollution and noise we have to endure today.

About the year 1901 I came across two captivating little organ pieces written by a blind composer, William Wolstenholme, who was organist in Blackburn, where he had been born. They appealed to me so much that I showed them to a close friend of mine, Stanley

Hawley, composer and pianist, who was at that time the honorary secretary of the Philharmonic Society. We played these charming compositions together, with the result that Hawley agreed with me we should ferret out this blind man and play to him his compositions, which I had arranged for viola and piano.

We found him in a modest home in which was an antiquated piano practically a semi-tone flat, a pitch not helpful to the tone quality of my viola. However Wolstenholme accompanied me in the pieces most delightfully and he so bubbled over with excitement that I had to repeat one of them, an *Allegretto*, three or four times before he would let me off.

We were so charmed with his demeanour that when Hawley and I returned home we decided that a position for him must be found in London; it was not right that a talented composer and excellent organist should be hidden away in Lancashire. Eventually, through Hawley's efforts, we obtained the post for him of organist at the Norfolk Square Church in Paddington, and he lived in London, with his sister who devoted her life to him, until his death in 1931. Wolstenholme in his early days had been a student at the Worcester College for the Blind and had had lessons on the violin from Elgar who was teaching there. I understand he was a very apt pupil and that Elgar took a great liking to him, so much so that when Wolstenholme sat for his Bachelor of Music examination, Elgar with his kindly good nature travelled with him to Oxford to act as his amanuensis. I gather that this was the first time a blind man had achieved this degree.

One of the most fortunate days for me occurred in 1902 when I met Miss Ada Gawthrop who was to become my wife. We met at Stafford House (which later became the London Museum) and again a little later at a concert given by the London Diocesan Orchestra in which she played the viola. This orchestra consisted of about forty women players, mostly amateurs, and was conducted by the talented amateur musician Margaret Haweis, sister of the Rev. H. R. Haweis, author of *Music and Morals*. The orchestra played well under her baton, and gave concerts in all the poorer districts of London – a good deal in the East End. One day my wife-to-be came to the Royal Academy where I was teaching and asked me to give her viola lessons, a proposal to which I readily assented. Often after we were married I would tell her that Stafford House had been the cause of her 'downfall'.

I occupied the principalship of the viola section in the Queen's Hall Orchestra until 1904. One day Robert Newman, manager of the orchestra, came to the platform during a rehearsal and made a revolutionary announcement. He told us in a few words that henceforward no deputies would be allowed to play. The deputy system had long been the bane of orchestral playing in London. The story goes that a player once sent to the first rehearsal of a concert a deputy, who in his turn sent a deputy to the second rehearsal, and this deputy's deputy turned up at the concert! The excuse if there was one for this paradoxical state of things was that by present-day standards players were miserably paid and were irresistibly tempted to accept the most remunerative job that was going. True, the system probably helped towards quick reading – English orchestral players were well known for being the best sight readers. But what a shameful situation, all the same. Newman's announcement led to an historic secession. Some forty of Henry Wood's players refused to relinquish their old privilege. They resigned and set about organizing a self-governing orchestra, the London Symphony. I was invited to join them as their principal viola, but I declined and at the same time relinquished my position in the Queen's Hall Orchestra. Before this happened I had made up my mind to give up orchestral playing as soon as possible and devote all my time to solo work. The Queen's Hall crisis was my opportunity. On the one hand I was devoted to Henry Wood, and on the other was attached to my colleagues who had seceded. By renouncing orchestral playing altogether I hoped to avoid hurting the feelings of either party.

I had greatly benefited by my experience as a member of Wood's orchestra. I learnt from him what good phrasing was, the accurate value of notes and of rests, and many another detail of help to musicianship, not to speak of discipline and punctuality. Wood was a man of active mind and great vitality, with a prodigious capacity for work. He was a martinet, as he had need to be to get through all the enterprises he undertook. Himself punctual to a fault, he could not forgive time-wasting in others. Years later I came into touch with him at a B.B.C. studio concert, where I was to play a viola concerto. Through faulty office-work I had been given the wrong time for the rehearsal and Wood had already begun. He stopped the orchestra to upbraid me, and would not be placated by my explanations that it was not my fault. All through the rehearsal of the work I was performing he was morose, and found cause to reprimand me at any or no provocation. Something he said at last cut me to the quick. At one point in the work the first oboe and I had to play one or two B flats in unison. Wood turned suddenly to me and said: 'Intonation! Intonation! Your B flat is sharp!' To me that accusation was a red rag to a bull. I exploded with rage. All my life I have concentrated on true intonation, and I flattered myself on being pretty good at it. The orchestra stopped, and I played a succession of B flats all down bows – crescendo, forte, fortissimo. Then I bellowed: 'That's my B flat, and there's nothing wrong with it! Ask your oboe-player about *his* B flat!' At this H.J.W. retorted, in his high-pitched counter-tenor voice: 'HOITY TOITY!' Things calmed down after that, the rehearsal continued without untoward interruption and I forgave what I considered a gross indignity. I was fond of H.J.W. and that night we gave a good performance. Nobody could steer one through a work better than he could.

I remember during the early years of my professorship at the R.A.M., about 1906, I was asked by the Principal to take into my class of students a young man of nineteen or twenty who came from Hucknall in Nottinghamshire. From the moment I heard him at his first lesson, I spotted that here was the nucleus of a good viola-player even though his efforts were rather crude, and I took an interest in him at once. His demeanour was of a charming, meek nature, but I was soon to learn that his pecuniary circumstances were of slender proportions, and I recollect that whenever I was able, I invited him to take lunch with me and saw to it that he had a good nourishing meal, for he always looked so fragile.

He did indeed turn out to be one of my best pupils and eventually became principal viola in the Henry J. Wood Queen's Hall Orchestra. I can't remember how long he held on to this position, but when the reader hears that he forsook the viola in order to engage in a far more remunerative occupation, that of composing music of a light character in which he excelled and became world-famous, they will not be surprised to learn that his name was Eric Coates. How right he was – for however efficiently he developed as a viola-player, and he played extremely well, he could never have achieved such a level of eminence, and certainly not of affluence, if he had got to the top of the tree as a viola soloist. His characteristic style of light music gave pleasure to myriads of listeners.

Some time between 1907 and 1908 a pedagogue with whom I became acquainted, Professor Willy Hess, master of a wonderfully

clean and miraculous technique, had become a professor at the
R.A.M. when I was teaching there. He immediately formed a string
quartet and asked me to be a member. In 1908 he invited me to go
with him to the United States to join a string quartet he was forming there. My aptitude for business has always been underdeveloped
and off I went without a contract. My first experience of the great
Republic was brief. On arriving at Boston, Mass., I found that the
terms offered to me were vastly inferior to those I had been promised
verbally in London. The American prospect, I decided, was unin-
viting, and exactly three weeks after arriving, I departed from New
York for home in the S.S. *Lusitania*. It is only right to admit there
was another factor in my decision. I was homesick and longing for
England, having become engaged to Ada before leaving.

Soon after my return to England, I was invited by the well-
known pianist, Katherine Goodson, to a party she was giving in
honour of that fine Hungarian composer Ernst von Dohnanyi, whom
it was a great pleasure for me to meet. In the course of conversation
I told him that I had played his C sharp minor sonata, exactly as
written for violin, many times in public. His reply was: 'Good
Heavens, how could you get up so high on the viola?' 'Well,' I said,
'I wish I had my viola here and we could play it together.' To which
Katherine Goodson interposed: 'I have not only the sonata but my
husband possesses a viola.' (Her husband was Arthur Hinton, also
a composer and a professor at the R.A.M.) Thereupon Dohnanyi sat
down at the piano and we played his C sharp minor violin sonata on
our first introduction, without rehearsal, and on a larger viola than
I had ever played on before! It was a most exciting performance for
me, as Dohnanyi, besides being a world-famous composer, was a
magnificent pianist.

4

Hobbies

In the early 1900s I became interested in the then rather crude motor-cycle and in due course saved up enough to enable me to purchase a second-hand machine. It had no gear changes in any shape or form. I was a complete ignoramus concerning anything mechanical and knew nothing about carburettors, correct vaporization of petrol, plug points, sooting-up, etc. All I knew was that the sharp downward pressure of the foot pedal ought to bring the motor to life. For the first few days, trying to accomplish this, I managed to get the wretched thing to fire now and then, but I usually found myself in a state of utter exhaustion with very little enthusiasm to do anything more than timidly allow the vehicle to take me a few yards. However, it was not very long before I decided on my first adventure; I hoped that it would carry me from Belmont, Sutton in Surrey, where I lived, to Guildford via Leatherhead.

I bowled along the road merrily until just beyond Leatherhead and over the bridge, where we were – the motor cycle and myself – confronted by a long steep hill leading to Albury. I had looked forward to this, but evidently the motor-cycle had not, for it took fright, stopped, and refused to budge an inch further. Do what I would, I could not get it to fire again. I had to push the heavy contrivance all the way up this very steep hill in free wheel, eventually arriving at the top of Albury Common utterly prostrate. I lay down on the grass, oblivious of the lovely view, in an effort to recover.

After a few minutes I managed to stagger to my feet, looking at my machine and wondering what I should do next, when to my joy a motor-cyclist appeared over the brow of the hill and parked his machine a few yards away. I went over to him and implored him to come to my assistance and bring my machine back to life. He was a very knowledgeable motor-cyclist and generously gave me some hints and tips, showing me that the plug points were solidly blocked

26

with soot owing to too much oil in the crank case, and next, that the petrol had overflowed the carburettor – the result of too high a level of float in it – coupled with maladjustment of the handle bar controls, etc. No machine on earth could have been expected to do its duty with such grievous defects.

After attending to these faults the friendly motor-cyclist sat on the saddle and with the first kick of the pedal brought the engine to life with explosions that were music to my ears. I returned home without contretemps, pompously feeling like a conquering hero. Needless to say I forthwith obtained an instruction book and acquainted myself with *my* duties to a motor-propelled bicycle. After this it bore me bravely to many of my professional engagements in town – at far less cost than the ordinary mode of travel, which was a consideration for me at that time.

In these early days of my musical activities there were quite a number of amateur instrumentalists who formed themselves into string quartets, trios, etc. and indulged in regular weekly practices of the classics in private. The only trouble, as ever, was the scarcity of violists, and as a consequence I was often roped in as a professional. One weekly engagement that I enjoyed was the Oxford and Cambridge Music Club, consisting entirely of undergraduates, whose club premises they owned in a lovely house in Bedford Square, London. The club was open daily – solely for ensemble playing and the delight of reading chamber music at sight. It also possessed a very large and comprehensive library.

Another weekly practice took place at 4 Chelsea Embankment, the home of Major Sir William Evans Gordon, an enthusiastic and capable amateur cellist. Sir William was the third husband of the Marchioness of Tweeddale who was also herself very fond of music. Sir William was a delightful man, bubbling over with musical enthusiasm. At these meetings he always invited a few friends interested in music as audience. On one occasion, when I was a mile or two from home on my way to Sir William, down pelted a torrent of rain which persisted all the way to Chelsea Embankment. Fortunately I always carried on the back of my motorcycle adequate equipment to protect me in such circumstances. I duly arrived at Sir William's house clad in sou'wester, knee-length leggings and waterproof wide-brimmed hat, including of course my viola case which was strapped obliquely across my back under my capacious sou'wester. When I rang the bell, who should open the door but Sir William himself, and when he saw me he exploded with laughter and insisted that I should come straight into the drawing-room and present myself to his friends without disrobing – I looked more like a member of a life-boat crew than a professional viola-player in my dripping raiment. He took me in just as I was, saying: 'Allow me to introduce the celebrated viola-player – Mr Lionel Tertis!' Having acquiesced in his whim I forthwith divested myself of my voluminous waterproof garments and returned to the drawing-room eager for music-making.

I was very active at this time except for twinges of rheumatism now and then which led me to seek palliatives. My search finally resulted in a visit to the then little-known Welsh spa of Llandrindod Wells, the waters there having been recommended to me as effective for this malady with which so many of us are afflicted. The outcome of my first visit to such a delightful part of the country was that it became an annual one for many years. Llandrindod Wells if I remember rightly is partly surrounded by hills, and my first peregrination led me through a very steep woodland path, on the top of which I found the Llandrindod Golf Club, situated on a plateau offering a most magnificent vista of undulating countryside for miles around.

The turf of this course was of velvety springy grass with greens of billiard-table character. It was not long before I became a much more enthusiastic golfer, with the result that I asked to be enrolled as a member of the club. I have had two hobbies in my life – golf and motoring. I never missed my daily round of eighteen holes, and stiff uphill walk, during my annual three weeks' course of 'taking the waters'. Eventually, after a few visits there and practice at my home course, I so improved my game that I achieved the proud handicap of nine at the Banstead Club, the first tee of which was only about forty yards from my home at Belmont. So enthusiastic was I that I remember that even snow in Banstead would not deter me from playing a round with a red ball, and on one occasion I completed two rounds in one day in the snow!

On one of my visits to Llandrindod I entered an open golf competition for a silver cup against all comers – which I won. My final opponent was a plus-one man! But let me hasten to say that I thoroughly demoralized him by my accurate one-handed putting on the greens (there was no rule against using one hand). I had no fewer than six one-putts on six of the greens in that final round of eighteen holes. My one-hand putt was deadly, no matter whether it was near or distant from the hole.

I was now thoroughly immersed in my hobby, to the point of neglecting my viola practice. The realization of this brought me up with a jerk. Curbing my ardour in this healthy exercise, I came back to my senses and to my duty to the viola—and bang went my Hobby No. 1.

During my annual visits to Llandrindod I also became interested in a motor-car showroom which specialized in the Ford car. It was very early days for the horseless carriage and the Ford looked more like an elongated spider than the body of a car, the top of it was so high. This early specimen, the Ford 'Model T', so fascinated me that eventually I plucked up courage and dipped my hands deep into my pockets, spending most of my savings to purchase one. Thus I became the proud owner of a much more convenient and comfortable method of propulsion than the rough and ready motor-cycle.

After two or three short lessons on the driving of the vehicle I pulled myself together and undertook the adventure of driving it back home. In those days macadamized roads were a rarity, and the by-roads consisted principally of loose gravel, etc. Ada and I were bowling along merrily at the excessive speed of 18 mph, when in the distance ahead of us we saw a man walking with his dray-horse and farm cart. When we got nearer to him he put up his hand. We stopped, wondering what was amiss, and as he came alongside he said in a quiet voice: 'I don't like dust!' We had been unaware that behind us we were raising clouds of it, and only then did we realize that in passing other vehicles we must be courteous and resist travelling at such a fantastic speed!

We eventually arrived at Henley-on-Thames. The exit from the town was over a bridge, after which we were faced with a long steep hill. We were about three-quarters of the way up when suddenly the engine stopped firing. I managed to apply hand and foot brakes pretty quickly, and there we were, stuck fast. I had had little or no experience of reversing the car, but very gingerly I released both brakes gradually to enable me to proceed backwards inch by inch. I think it must have taken me quite a quarter of an hour to get back to the bridge at the bottom of the hill, all the time having to turn my head, looking over the extreme right of my shoulder as far as my neck could possibly permit, with the result that I felt I had dislocated that part of my anatomy by the time we reached the bottom. However, Ada quickly walked over the bridge to a near-by garage and returned with one of the mechanics. With a mighty heave from the three of us we managed to push the car to the garage where it was discovered that the magneto was the culprit. This was soon put right and we gained the top of the hill in triumph. But I had to put up with a stiff neck for a couple of days afterwards as a reward for my first experience of being the driver of a motor-car for a distance of 170 miles from Wales to London, and this I did with equanimity.

As usual never going half-way, I soon began trying to ferret out the mechanics of my new toy, both inside the bonnet and underneath the chassis on my back – spending far too much time on the vehicle, with the result of course that again my viola suffered. So eventually bang went Hobby No. 2.

Such are the sacrifices of an interpreter of music, but one suffers them gladly. It is well worth it.

5

The Young Mr Beecham–and New English Composers

In spite of my resolution not to devote any more time to orchestral playing, I did after all return to it for a short period, being unable to resist an offer from the then young Thomas Beecham to play as principal viola in a small orchestra he was forming, to be led by Albert Sammons. I say 'the young Beecham'; but in a sense the word is superfluous, for Beecham was a man who never grew old. What a fountain of musical genius, charm and exuberant spirits he always was. People will no doubt continue to try their hands at recording his career, but the cleverest pen will never recapture the sparkle of his music-making or the wit of his speech. Once and once only did I know him speechless. A German tenor who went by the name of Tamini sang at a number of concerts during a provincial tour undertaken by the Beecham orchestra (this was in 1909), and the incident occurred in a hotel at Preston after our performance. Tamini, evidently full of enthusiasm for Beecham's conducting of the aria he had sung, suddenly flung his arms round his neck and fervently embraced him. Unforgettable for me was Beecham's face and look of horror. Words failed him . . . I regret to have to say that poor Tamini was made to pay for his indiscretion. A heartless plot was hatched. After he had retired to his top-floor bedroom it was arranged that a message should be sent to his room to the effect that he was wanted on the telephone – his wife had put through an urgent call from London. Down he came in agitation and a dressing-gown, and while he was wrestling with the telephone, members of the orchestra raided his room and flung his dress clothes out of the window. It was a rainy night. There was a sequel to this wicked folly. Tamini complained to the police, and the next morning, at Preston Junction station, our train was delayed – much to the station-master's annoyance – while detectives questioned the players.

They were unsuccessful with their enquiries, and meanwhile the station-master most vehemently expressed his irritation. The orchestra determined to reprove him for his lack of urbanity by letting off fireworks whenever we passed through Preston Junction station, as we frequently did. The last time we did it we provided a most imposing display, and earned in Lancashire the name 'the fireworks orchestra'. It was a very young orchestra.

I remember one concert we gave in Liverpool, when Beecham and a few of us stayed at the Adelphi hotel. At that time it was old and out of date and there was a spiral staircase to all floors with central chandeliers containing electric bulbs, all of which were easily reached by hand on each landing. The high-spirited Beecham was particularly pleased with the success of the concert we had given that night, we were in the best of spirits at the supper afterwards, and it was well beyond midnight before the conclusion of the meal. Beecham, Sammons, Warwick Evans (principal cellist) and I then retired to our rooms. We did not deign to take the lift but tripped up the five or six floors of the staircase in jovial mood. At each landing Beecham surreptitiously withdrew an electric bulb from the chandeliers. Sammons, Evans and I were not in a condition to realize what Beecham was up to, but we soon found out when we reached the top landing where our bedrooms were situated, for Beecham immediately dropped all the bulbs he had collected down the central aperture of the staircase – they fell to the ground floor with a tremendous explosion!

The resultant chaos in the hotel can well be imagined – doors of bedrooms were flung open and I could see the night-porter flying upstairs. The wily Beecham was first into his bedroom, and Sammons also reached his before the porter arrived at the top floor, but Warwick Evans and I were caught. I can't remember whether the police were called or not, but in the morning all was well. Beecham poured oil on troubled waters and 'paid the piper'.

Beecham imposed himself on one and all by his instinctive musicianship and brilliance. From the first he was a leader of men. Already in his youth he possessed a magnetic influence to draw out the best in his players. How much the musical world has owed to his marvellous gifts. Sometimes it is suggested that fire and exciting impetuosity were his great characteristics, but that is not enough to say: equally important in his art was his command of subtle nuances, especially in Mozart, with realizations of supreme loveliness. And

I know of no other conductor who could so fully reflect the poetry of Delius's music, his thrilling exquisite harmonization and moving ethereal melodies of transcendent beauty, as did Sir Thomas.

My year with Beecham was an interlude. My own vocation was calling me, and soon I was back on the platform as a soloist – an obstinate, ill-rewarded, never-to-be-discouraged viola soloist, in the days when most people had not heard a viola solo in their lives. I would give as many as six recitals in a London season, with programmes largely made up of new English music. Those were times when the native muse was largely out of favour, and I have the satisfaction of knowing that the formation of the British Music Society was the result of my persistence in playing British music as much as possible. Stanley Hawley, secretary of the Royal Philharmonic Society, was my principal supporter in this movement.

From the beginning of my campaign to create a library of solo viola music I begged for viola compositions from the younger English composers; and great is my debt to them. Such was their response that the British library of viola music looked like becoming the most extensive in the world; as a result, in course of time, foreign composers also became interested and wrote for the solo viola. In my young days only two major works for the viola with orchestra by great masters existed, Berlioz's *Harold in Italy* and Mozart's Sinfonia Concertante. The latter enchanting work had lain for generations unknown to all but scholars; the world in general had not heard of its existence. Even as late as 1924, when I played in it with Kreisler at the Albert Hall, the newspapers came out with such phrases as: 'Mozart's rarely heard Concertante . . . containing some of Mozart's most superlative music', 'This little-known work', 'These men played a practically unknown Concertante of Mozart.'

It was pure generosity in those days at the beginning of the century to write for the solo viola. Publishers would not consider anything of the sort, to them it was a distinctly bad commercial proposition. However, my composer friends continued to write a number of works for me. The style of their music belongs to the period, but it was beautiful, and was a powerful influence in the advancement of the viola. Benjamin Dale and York Bowen were the first to make contributions to the new solo literature, followed soon after by Arnold Bax. These three were all students at the

R.A.M. at about the same time, around 1900, and goaded by my constant pressure for works for the viola, they provided the beginning of a library with music for viola and piano and viola and orchestra.

Of York Bowen and his compositions for the viola I have already spoken. One of the first works of major importance was the Suite for viola and piano by Benjamin Dale, consisting of three movements (Dale later, at my request, arranged the second and third movements for viola and orchestra). The middle movement is entitled 'Romance' and contains a lovely continuous melody of no fewer than thirty-eight bars. The title 'Romance' partly fails to imply the significance and import of this beautiful, long and varied movement which I have often played as my only contribution in programmes of orchestral symphony concerts. The middle section of it consists of elaborate, intricate and brilliant technical passage-work in which rubato is of such cunning and so incessant that it requires a conductor of very considerable experience to follow and be on the spot. Dale was a greatly gifted but strangely reticent musician. Something in his character, something finical, ultra-fastidious seemed as time went on to check his creative impulse, and the high hopes entertained for his future were disappointed.

The first performance of Dale's Suite in its orchestral garb, which took place on 18 May 1911 with Nikisch conducting, was a nightmare. The famous conductor, secure in his immense reputation, had not taken the slightest trouble to acquaint himself with the work, and he gave us a casual, hasty and utterly inadequate rehearsal. Such was the attitude, still tolerated in 1911, of a lordly foreigner towards the native muse. This concert was my second appearance for the Philharmonic Society. My first had been on 26 March 1908 when I introduced York Bowen's concerto for viola and orchestra with Landon Ronald conducting. In all, I played at eleven Royal Philharmonic Society concerts.

Arnold Bax wrote many orchestral works, including seven symphonies. He was also extremely prolific in chamber music, and composed a number of works of that category for me. One of the best he ever wrote is the sonata for viola and piano.

There has always been a myth about Bax that he was Irish; he was not. But he was very fond of Ireland and often visited the southern part. My association with him began at the R.A.M. He was very shy and reticent, and although an extremely good pianist he rarely played in public. He frequently changed his address, principally around north London, but eventually he decided he would get away from the tumult and find a peaceful place in the country where he could work undisturbed. This turned out to be a pub in the village of Storrington, Sussex, about ten miles from Worthing. His room was in a quiet part of the building and here he became a recluse and could not be got at by anyone when he was composing – but at opening time he could usually be found in the bar parlour with a tankard of ale, smoking his pipe, in animated conversation with the village farm workers. I seem to remember that he was reputed to be an excellent cricketer, both batsman and bowler. Indeed, when I was staying in Bath in 1938 he came there as a member of an amateur team to play against the County Cricket Club.

Besides the viola sonata Bax wrote a *Legend* for viola and harp, a trio for flute, viola and harp, and in 1920 a concerto for viola and orchestra which he later called a *Phantasy*. I gave the last-mentioned its first performance under Albert Coates at the Queen's Hall on 17 November 1921.

Other first performances in which I was later involved as viola soloist with orchestra were those of the following: Vaughan Williams's *Flos Campi* (November 1925 under Henry Wood; I gave a second performance with Henry Wood on 3 November 1927 for the Royal Philharmonic Society); my arrangement of Elgar's cello concerto (21 March 1930, the composer conducting); Vaughan Williams's Suite (12 November 1934 under Malcolm Sargent); Holst's *Lyric Movement* (18 March 1934 under Adrian Boult); T. F. Dunhill's *Triptych* (19 August 1942 under Boult); Richard Walthew's *Mosaic in Ten Pieces* (10 July 1943 under Clarence Raybould). I am proud that these and other works should have been dedicated to me.

Another young composer I got to know in the early 1900s was Percy Grainger. Born in Australia, he lived in London for about fifteen years before settling in America and becoming a naturalized American. He was a brilliant pianist, and I became very friendly with him. More than once I went backstage to listen when he was giving a recital or playing a concerto. Before he was due to go on to the platform he would invariably slap his knees ferociously for at least half a minute and the noise he made could be heard many yards away. When I asked him why he did it he said: 'To make my blood run fast and give me courage.' He made a point of never using Italian musical terms – in his scores he always wrote his marks of expression in English. Instead of *molto crescendo* he would write *louden lots*. During his stay in London he was most interested in English folk music, and we all know of his delightful compositions in this category, such as 'Molly on the Shore', 'Handel in the Strand', etc. He was ever a most exhilarating companion.

The impression of him that remains in my mind is of his always being chock-a-block full of masculine strength and spriteliness. I remember in New York my apartment was a good many floors up, but he would never deign to take the lift no matter how high he had to climb; instead he would leap up the staircase at full speed two steps at a time to arrive panting at my door. On one occasion – whether in London or America I cannot remember – he invited me to come to a railway station to meet his fiancée. While walking up and down the platform he sang a tune, bouche fermée, a strange sort of noise to my ears to say the least of it, and when I asked him what it was he replied that it had just come to him, that he would write it out and dedicate it to me for unaccompanied solo viola and would give it the title 'A Platform Humlet'. However, when I received the manuscript and played it through it sounded so devastatingly ugly that I never performed it either in private or public – neither do I remember to what infernal end I consigned it!

One work of which I did *not* give the first performance was Walton's masterly concerto. With shame and contrition I admit that when the composer offered me the first performance I declined it. I was unwell at the time; but what is also true is that I had not learnt to appreciate Walton's style. The innovations in his musical language, which now seem so logical and so truly in the main-stream of music, then struck me as far-fetched. It took me time to realize what a tower of strength in the literature of the viola is this concerto, and how deep the gratitude that we who play the viola should feel towards the composer – the gratitude, too, to Beecham for having suggested to Walton the composition of a viola concerto for me. I remember that, when Walton came to me with it and I refused the honour, he was generous enough not to seem to take it too much amiss but asked me to suggest someone else to undertake the performance. I immediately thought of Paul Hindemith, a well-known and much-talked-of composer and a viola-player too. So it was that Hindemith played the work for the first time at Queen's Hall. I was a member of the audience, and felt great disappointment with his playing. The notes, certainly, were all there, but the tone was cold and unpleasing and the instrument he played did not deserve to be called a viola, it was far too small.

Later on a chance was offered to me to play a concerto by Hindemith himself. In a letter from the Berlin Philharmonic Orchestra it was suggested that it would be pleasing for a British viola-player to play the composition of a German composer who was himself a viola soloist. I perused the score and found that most of it was crammed with fiendishly difficult passage-work – a technique that was peculiarly his own and which he himself played marvellously. It was not music to me, and I reluctantly had to refuse the offer.

The Berlin Philharmonic Orchestra, conducted by Furtwängler, gave one or two highly successful concerts in London about this time, and the public appeared to be inordinately captivated. I was not in London at the time, being in Berlin myself preparing for a viola recital. While there I was keen to hear them and took the opportunity of going to one of their concerts on their return to Berlin, looking forward to great things after all I had heard about their performances at home. I was so disappointed that I did not sit the programme out. No doubt they were well disciplined; but it was the coldest playing I had ever heard in my life, particularly on the part of the strings. And the brass was blatant. Not that I have ever considered our own string players to be as warm in their playing as they might be. I put *their* deficiency down to the traditional suppression of emotional expression which in the course of generations has become part of the English character. But hang it all! How is the sound of a contraption of wood and gut, etc. to be made worth listening to, if one does not bring to bear every ounce of vitality and emotional sensibility of which one is capable? All the same, our orchestral string players were infinitely more expressive than the Berliners of that time.

On my return home from Berlin, Ada and I were married at Epsom Registry Office, and Margaret Haweis was a witness. We went to live in a small house at Belmont, then an outpost in the country: cows grazed in fields just beyond our garden, where the Sutton by-pass now runs. Going home after evening concerts, as the last train for Belmont left Victoria at about eight o'clock, I had to get off at Sutton, which was on the main line to Portsmouth, and walk a mile and a half to Belmont.

6

1914–18

My memory now brings me with awful remembrance and shock to one of the horrible blots in world history – the war of 1914–18 that was to impoverish and disrupt the progress of civilization such as we glibly supposed it to be. Whatever our apprehensions, we little realized that it would spell the end of the sanguine, prosperous, hopefully forward-looking Europe most of us regarded as becoming solidly established – a civilization capable of improvement of course, but at the same time representing the highest degree so far attained in the foibles of humanity's efforts.

In due course I was called up for military service, was placed in category C.3 owing to my health and appointed a Special Constable. When I was not patrolling I was posted to guard a reservoir, by the side of which there was a hut where I used to practise surreptitiously on my viola with a heavy brass mute in order to subdue the tone. My inspector, when he came along, would wink the other eye. Now and then I would be released from duty in order to give recitals at various cathedrals, which I had organized for war charities.

Early in the war many Belgian refugees came to England. Among them was a most excellent violinist Désiré Defauw, a fine cellist Emile Doehaerd, and Joseph Jongen, a composer and pianist and head of the Liège Conservatoire. I joined with these three to form the 'Belgian Piano Quartet'. Defauw was always full of amusing stories. He spoke English very well but was quick to poke fun at his compatriots who did not. The wife of one of them was suddenly taken ill, and the husband sent a young member of the family to telephone the doctor – the message was – 'Tell the doctor he must can come quick if he can't!' Then there was a foreign conductor of poor capability with still less knowledge of the English language who was rehearsing a very experienced small English orchestra. The players became so bored with his bad musicianship that they began

talking during the rehearsal, poco a poco crescendo until the conductor exploded with exasperation and bellowed to the leader
(who was the worst offender): 'You no shpoke – you went!'

The great Belgian violinist Ysaye (Ysaÿe, as his name should
strictly speaking be spelt) was also a refugee in London, and I often
enjoyed making music with him. He and I played Mozart's *Sinfonia
Concertante* at Queen's Hall on 28 February 1916, with Beecham
conducting. Ysaye promised to write a cadenza for this performance
but he did not finish it in time. Years passed and I had forgotten all
about it, and it was not until 1950 that I received from the great
violinist's son Antoine the manuscript of the cadenza he had
promised, inscribed: 'A mon ami Lionel Tertis'. But it turned out
to be interminably long and frightfully difficult technically; because
of its length alone I doubt if anyone would ever have played it. I
returned it to Antoine for his archives.

Ysaye was a glorious artist, with a tone of prodigious volume and
inordinate technical powers. He was a huge man, and he smoked a
correspondingly huge pipe; even his match-boxes were outsize; and
his hat had the widest brim I had ever seen. He attracted attention
wherever he went. Only his violin was of standard dimensions, and
in his hands it looked a toy. I retain a vivid memory of his leading
the most exciting performance of César Franck's quintet I have ever
known. He took the finale at a terrific pace . . . inspiring, exhilarating,
wonderful. Those who heard him only towards the end of his life
know but the shadow of his art. Among his compositions are six
sonatas for solo violin, one of which, the fourth, he dedicated to
Kreisler. Philip Newman, an outstanding fiddler and a pupil of
Ysaye, told me that he stood outside the bedroom door on the day
Ysaye died in 1931 and played this sonata to him. He was afterwards informed by Antoine Ysaye that his father opened his eyes
when he heard the violin and at the end of the first movement murmured 'Very fine!' During the finale Ysaye tried to beat time and
when the sonata came to an end he said, 'Splendid! – but a little too
fast.' Those were the last words he spoke.

I call to mind a private rehearsal of the Mozart *Sinfonia Concertante* with Ysaye at Queen's Hall the day before the Beecham concert, at which Ysaye arranged all the phrasing he wanted. This went
as planned at the orchestral rehearsal the next morning but un-
accountably he radically altered a good deal of his phrasing at the
performance at night! As some of my readers probably know, the

phrases of the Concertante are very similar for the solo instruments – question and answer so to speak, and I had to copy him on the spur of the moment. Phew! After the performance, just off the platform, I suddenly found two great saucer-eyes quite close to my face, and a stentorian voice said, 'Well down! Well down!' Voice and saucer-eyes belonged to that picturesque and adorable Spanish cellist Augustin Rubio, who had lived in England for years but could never get his pronunciation or his English right. The next day I had a letter from him:

> My dear Monarch and friend Tertis,
>   I send you with my congratulations for your 'perfect' rendering of Mozart 'Concertante' the notice in the *Pall Mall Gazette*. Hoping you find at last your beautiful bed in the proper way to take a COLOSSAL rest,
>   I send you both my love.
>   Augustin Rubio

Some days later a message came to Ysaye from Lord Curzon whose country home was Hackwood near Basingstoke, saying that the little daughter of the Queen of the Belgians was staying with them and asking him whether he would come and make some music. Arthur Rubinstein was in London, and Ysaye collected three others to form a quintet – Albert Sammons, Emile Doehaerd and myself. We went down for the day and were greeted and delightfully entertained by Lady Ravensdale, Lord Curzon's daughter. We played chamber music galore but so engrossed were we all (including our host) that we overlooked the clock and missed the last London train. So at Hackwood we spent the night, kitless. Lord Curzon produced one unused toothbrush which he put up for auction among the five of us. He lent me a suit of his pyjamas – the pyjamas of a much taller man than myself, and of far greater girth, which necessitated my employing many folds in the garment. How the other members of the quintet fared, history does not relate.

In that year the King and Queen of the Belgians invited Ysaye to go over to La Panne – situated in the narrow strip of unoccupied Belgium – to play to them and others near the battle-front. Ysaye invited me to join the party. This visit lasted for seven days, and for me the experience of having been so near the dreadful theatre of war, thoughts of which preoccupied men's minds for four wearing

years, is something never to be forgotten. I kept a naive diary, and
here is some of it.

June 16, 1916. 1st day. Left my home at Belmont, Surrey at
6.15 a.m. Travelled to Victoria and on to Charing Cross, where
on the platform I met Rousseau, the Belgian poet, and soon
after Ysaye and a Major Gordon (Courier to the King and
Queen of the Belgians), Emile Doehaerd the cellist and Theo,
Ysaye's brother – a pianist.

We arrived at Folkestone at 10.45 a.m. and embarked with
hundreds of soldiers. The first thing that greeted us was a
submarine partly submerged. The boat departed at 11.30 a.m.
and all had to wear life-belts. After we had gone a little way out
scores of merchant ships crossed our path – they looked like a
long avenue as far as the eye could see sailing towards Dover.
We were escorted by a torpedo boat. When we arrived at
Boulogne harbour we saw the masts of one of our ammunition
ships protruding above the water. It had been torpedoed eight
months before by a German submarine. We disembarked, and
our little party with Major Gordon at the head passed through
all the sentries and officials with no trouble. A royal car was
waiting for us and we were five inside and two outside – a
pretty good pack. We had not driven many miles before we
were held up at a barrier by a sentinel with fixed bayonet –
altogether we were stopped fifteen times between Boulogne
and La Panne, our destination, but we passed through every
check point with the greatest ease – Major Gordon saw to that.
There were innumerable English soldiers in camps as we
motored at the merry pace of 35 mph over vile roads. We
stopped at Calais and met Antoine, Ysaye's youngest son, in
khaki. The boy went away rejoicing from Papa with a 100 franc
note in his pocket. We arrived at 4.45 p.m. at La Panne where
we were to stay for a week.

At 6 p.m. an official car came for Ysaye and Rousseau to go
to the Queen. Soon after we received a note asking us (Theo,
Doehaerd and myself) to join Ysaye at the royal villa and bring
music and instruments at 8.30 p.m.

The great impression I had during the evening was of the
most delightful simplicity of their Majesties, and their gracious-
ness, added to which were their extraordinarily modest

surroundings. They lived in a simple villa overlooking the sea, plainly furnished, with an upright piano of questionable age. We began by playing a piano quartet by Fauré and then Ysaye asked me to play a solo, after which we finished with the Brahms G minor piano quartet. Then followed refreshments during the course of which King Albert said to me with a twinkle in his eye: 'I often see the Zeppelins going over to pay you a visit, in broad daylight.'

2nd day. Up at 8.30 a.m. No bell in my room and utmost difficulty in obtaining 'de l'eau chaud'. Major Gordon came to take us to play in a hospital. We drove through a market place like a town of the dead with nearly every building smashed to bits, and one could hear the guns at Ypres going on all the time. In this square a great review of troops had taken place some time back before King Albert and King George V. Just before we sat down to lunch there was a terrific bang and Ysaye said, 'There goes the dinner gong!' Afterwards we learned it was one of the largest German guns, known as the 'Big Bertha'. In the afternoon we played at one of the most important hospitals in what remained of Belgium, staffed by English nurses. The hospital depressed me very much – to see all those poor maimed fellows was rather overwhelming, and this represented so-called civilization. The next few days our tasks were similar – to play three or four times to gatherings of soldiers both fit and wounded, in the open, in ramshackle buildings or in tents. Some of the soldiers were wheeled in, in beds in front of the platform. The Queen came to every concert we gave and invariably brought her camera. She was a most enthusiastic photographer. At one of the concerts Prince Alexander of Teck came with the Queen. I was presented to him. He was very musical and loved the viola.

On the 6th day we walked on the sea front and saw one of the very latest aeroplanes – a chaser – doing some marvellous aerobatics. I was told it could fly at 200 mph, an incredible speed! At the last concert we played a string trio of Beethoven and we all played solos (Ysaye, Doehaerd and myself). Before we left Belgium I was escorted on a tour of the front line trenches; my equilibrium was somewhat shaken by seeing a shell explode rather too near to be comfortable. This was, needless to say, not a time of major operations in the north. It had so far been the year of the long-drawn-out agony of Verdun; and the fearful battle of the Somme was in preparation.

The journey home on the last day with a VIP officer in a royal car brought us to the harbour at Boulogne where our passports were examined. On board we found the boat crammed with soldiers going on leave. We were again in convoy escorted by a destroyer. I eventually reached home thrilled with my experience at the Belgian front.

On my return to England I resumed practising hard at my viola for I had to prepare for concerts. Unfortunately for me spring-cleaning was in progress at home, and the only room available was one in which our talkative parrot resided in her cage. I remember I was practising a beautiful phrase with all the soul and emotion I could put into it. During my fervour I was conscious of peculiar sounds going on in the room and looking up at the parrot, found to my consternation that she was in the process of being violently sick! The sight distinctly curbed my ardour and I must confess I slunk out of the room muttering: 'All right, old bird, that's the last time I'll play to you.'

In London that year Ysaye came to a recital of mine at the Aeolian Hall, situated in New Bond Street, where I played my G minor transposition of Bach's D minor Chaconne. To my astonishment and embarrassment he came on to the platform at the end of the performance and publicly embraced me! I should perhaps have mentioned before now that, after long preparation, I had taken my courage in both hands in 1911 and given the first performance in public of the Chaconne *on the viola*. I had practised it for years, and in the simplicity of my heart imagined that the audacious enterprise would make the viola talked about 'all over the town'. No doubt, I thought, the reaction would be that some, in those early days of my campaign, would denounce me for my sacrilege in daring to transpose it for the viola, while others, I hoped, would be favourably impressed and even enthusiastic. What happened was something for which I was totally unprepared – the first time in history, as far as I knew, that the Chaconne was performed on the viola was ignored by all the newspapers, except Edwin Evans (who became music critic of the *Pall Mall Gazette* in 1912 and later the *Daily Mail*) writing in a magazine called *The Outlook*. As a consequence of his commendation of my venture, I wrote the following letter to him, expressing my indignation pretty strongly at so little notice being taken of this big effort to attract attention to the viola.

Dear Mr Evans,

I can't thank you sufficiently for your article in *The Outlook*. It is so understanding, and fully realizes the shameful neglect of the viola as a solo instrument. The concert has been disgracefully treated as far as the press is concerned. All the London newspapers absolutely ignored it. I suppose if I had come from Bulgaria (or some other foreign country with an unpronounceable name) they would have taken more interest in it.

Surely they know by this time that my aim and object is not for any personal prestige in any way, but solely and purely for the furtherance of the claims of the viola as a solo instrument.

It is really very heart-breaking – the absolute indifference of the musical critics towards their own countrymen, no matter how sincere one's efforts are. I am so sick about it that I don't think it is worth while using up my vitality and spending the little money I can scrape together for the Cause in this country.

I am seriously thinking of devoting my efforts for the propagation of the viola as a solo instrument henceforth by giving recitals on the continent and in the USA, whenever I can get the cash together. I am sure much more good will come of it there.

Once more let me thank you most sincerely for your words of encouragement which have done more than anything to lift up my drooping spirits.

I also wrote a letter to my friend Frederick Corder who was a composer, and the then Curator at the Royal Academy of Music. In the course of it I told him what I had written to Edwin Evans and angrily suggested that my being British was the reason for the music critics' neglect of my Chaconne, and I threatened to go off to the continent and start a fresh career there. Corder was another disappointed man. In his reply he said:

Is it any consolation to know that others are suffering even more than yourself? I have had five such disappointments during the last fortnight, and if I were twenty years younger should certainly feel like chucking the whole thing up. As it is,

I endeavour to console myself with the belief that no really good effort is in vain. Such a performance as you gave the other night will long live in the memories of those who were present, and some good must come of it eventually.

During the First World War I took part in some of the most delightful chamber music making imaginable. The scene was a cellar in Chelsea, and the meetings lasted as a rule from midnight till daybreak! The audience were guests of an enthusiastic American music-lover, Muriel Draper. No public performances could ever have reached such a pitch of carefree, rapturous inspiration. There were no rehearsals; the music came fresh, and the executants were no duffers – they included Ysaye, Casals, Thibaud, Harold Bauer, Cortot, Kochanski (a brilliant Polish violinist), Szymanowski, Arbos, Arthur Rubinstein and Albert Sammons. Mrs Draper had built a basement room for music under her two houses (19 and 19a) in Edith Grove, Chelsea. We used to call it 'Mrs Draper's cellar'. Ysaye's word for it was 'le cave'. There were plenty of easy chairs, and huge cushions were strewn on the floor. At intervals delicious food was forthcoming. Out of the innumerable works performed, ranging from duets to octets, one in particular stands out in my memory: Brahms's C minor piano quartet, played by Ysaye, Casals, Rubinstein and myself. Prodigious, the lusciousness and wealth of sound! Ysaye with his great volume of tone and glorious phrasing, Casals playing in the slow movement with divinely pure expression, Rubinstein with his demoniacal command of the keyboard (his ferocity in the Scherzo was frightening) – what an experience for me to be associated with such giants.

It was my good fortune to meet Rubinstein when he was a young man in his twenties and I was in my thirties. He was a wonderful pianist at that time but had more leisure than in later years to devote to his friends, and I had the joy of making music with him on many occasions. From the numerous parties at which we gathered, a memory that is particularly impressed on my mind is of his extraordinary gift for playing excerpts from any symphony or opera that you cared to mention – a marvellous feat at which he never faltered.

In 1916 I enjoyed the excitement of playing at a concert with Ysaye and Vladimir de Pachmann, in Mozart's clarinet trio in E flat (the clarinet part on the viola). Just before we went on to the platform Pachmann put his arms round Ysaye and me – or as nearly round as they would go (both Pachmann and Ysaye were portly figures) – and in dulcet tones, with his beatific smile, said: 'We tree. . . !'

It was also my great privilege about this time to meet that most wonderful bass-baritone and fine artist Chaliapin, who was three years older than myself. Apart from our musical interests a most extraordinary sympathy developed between us, the cause of it being that an accident had happened to each of us in our youth with exactly similar consequences.

In my case, when I was eight years old, I was knocked down by a thief who was running away, and my face hit the pavement rather badly. In the course of our conversations, Chaliapin and I found we had both suffered nasal and antrum injuries of identical character, under similar circumstances, which had interrupted our studies over a period of years through recurring operations, major and otherwise. The medical fraternity at that time knew little about how to deal with faulty antrums. However, mercifully the remarkable sonority of Chaliapin's marvellous voice was not affected, and I myself managed to go on scraping the viola for a good seventy years more. Incidentally, this condition was the real cause of my being relegated to category C.3 in the 1914–18 War.

We in Britain did try to keep the arts going in spite of the holocaust, and I remember, to quote just one instance, Adrian Boult's first appearance in the Queen's Hall in February 1918. My participation in this concert was Benjamin Dale's Romance for viola and orchestra and the unaccompanied Bach Chaconne (which I played on the viola transposed a fifth down). What was indelibly impressed upon me was how, on this first occasion and the very many others when thereafter I made music with Adrian Boult, I always felt comfortable in any variations of tempi, dynamics and so on knowing that Boult's control of the orchestra would be co-ordinated with every whim of my personal reflection in the work I was playing.

Again during the First World War period I had the honour of meeting that great artist Ellen Terry. One day an opportunity came to take advantage of this acquaintance and I boldly wrote asking her if she would be patron for one of my charity concerts. She replied with a charming letter saying she would be delighted.

Not long before the First World War I had paid my second visit to the United States, which had consisted entirely of an extensive tour with the Harold Bauer Piano Quartet, the members being

Harold Bauer (piano), Bronislaw Huberman (violin), Felix Salmond (cello) and myself. The ordinary Pullman of an American train has a good-sized wash-house at either end, one for men and the other for women. Huberman was an insatiable man for practising, and on our journeys he would be found in the men's wash-house playing his violin from morning till night, meal-times excepted. He never stopped, no matter how many passengers were performing their ablutions, and how it came about that he was not forcibly restrained from turning the wash-house into a practice room I shall never understand.

After my most enjoyable participation in piano quartet performances during our tour in America, I returned home to be involved in a peculiar experience – being a member for a short time of the famous Bohemian String Quartet in London. As a result of an urgent appeal from Broadwood & Sons, the well-known piano manufacturers – who gave series of chamber music concerts at the Aeolian Hall in Bond Street and in the provinces – I was called upon to play with this celebrated quartet at a moment's notice, practically without rehearsal. The works included Schubert's great D minor quartet *Death and the Maiden*, and I shall never forget the furious pace at which they took the last movement – full of fire and meticulous articulation; indeed the whole quartet was played with sparkling rhythm and crystal-clear precision. Fortunately I knew this Schubert quartet extremely well and found myself able to fall in with their ideas. Whenever I hear this quartet now it reminds me of my association with the Czechs, the cause of which to say the least of it was somewhat irregular.

The urgent appeal for me to play with them was due, I was told, to their viola-player Nedbal, a very fine artist, having been suddenly taken ill. But to my amazement I discovered at the end of the tour that the remarkable and devastating reason for their viola-player's indisposition was that he had not in fact been indisposed at all, but had run off with the first violinist's wife!

Josef Hofman the leader was a virtuoso, Josef Suk the second violin was a composer, a charming man and an excellent player; but the cellist, a most magnificent executant, had the objectionable habit of expectorating frequently during the course of the day – so much so that I felt that his equipment should have included a spittoon! Apart from this my collaboration with the Bohemians was for me an exciting and wonderful musical experience.

My next venture in ensemble playing was of a more or less permanent nature, and took the shape of another piano quartet: Albert
Sammons the leader, William Murdoch pianist, Felix Salmond
cellist and myself. My wife christened us with the splendid title of
'The Chamber Music Players'. We made music together for the
best part of twenty-two years with only two changes (both cellists –
Cedric Sharp followed by Lauri Kennedy in place of Felix Salmond
who had gone to America). Some of the happiest hours of my life
were spent with these good friends and excellent musicians. We
had not been formed as a team for very long before our activities
were interrupted by the First World War. Sammons and Murdoch
were conscripted and joined the Grenadier Guards as musicians.
The first thing that happened to them, so Sammons later told me,
was to be gathered together with other raw recruits in a room at
Caterham barracks. In stalked the sergeant to address some preliminary remarks to them, and bawled out in a stentorian voice:
'Any musicians 'ere? – Put up yer 'ands.' Sammons and Murdoch
promptly did so. The sergeant continued: 'Come on, you two, I
want you to move a pianner!'

Whenever I could, I visited them in their barracks and made a
special effort to get to know the sergeant, cajoling him – with a
bottle of whisky now and then which I surreptitiously brought in –
to do his utmost to look after Sammons and Murdoch, for they were
two of our best-known musicians, and keep them off any tasks that
might injure their hands; this I eventually found he did to the best
of his ability.

I was not qualified either in stature or in health to join my
colleagues as a Grenadier Guardsman. Once, however, I posed as a
Grenadier when I offered to play with them to strengthen the viola
section at a concert the Grenadier band gave in the barracks. Sitting
amongst those brawny fellows I felt as if I were a puny mascot be-
longing to the regiment. It is my misfortune that a photograph pic-
turing us all on this occasion has been lost. Sammons and Murdoch
did not play their respective instruments in the orchestra but were
relegated to the clarinet section. I hasten to say that both of them
had only the very scantiest knowledge of the techniques of the
instrument and Heaven knows what sort of sounds were emitted!
I also remember the two being posted at times on guard outside
Buckingham Palace as part of their duties.

As soon as the awful 1914–18 War was over, the Chamber Music

Players continued with regular practice. The exhilaration of our being together again was a great enjoyment and satisfaction to us all. We worked hard to get into form once more but now and then at rehearsals we let off steam with hilarious fooling in which Sammons, so full of wit and humour, was the ringleader. One prank for which I was unashamedly accountable happened after we had practised very diligently the first movement of the G minor Fauré piano quartet. Before we started the slow movement I remarked to my companions that I felt tired and would lie down for five minutes. To their astonishment I proceeded to crawl under the piano with bow and viola, and lying flat on my back asked Murdoch to begin the slow movement, in which the viola joins the piano in a lovely melody marked pianissimo. I played this with exaggerated drawling, sickly portamenti, replete with faulty intonation, and had not proceeded very far when suddenly Murdoch hit the piano with a tremendous left-hand fortissimo chord low down in the bass which sounded to me in my position like a cannon shot. That put an end to my escapade and I crawled out from under the piano feeling as if I had concussion of the brain!

Having come to our senses after the surfeit of tomfoolery, we proceeded to rehearse again seriously. These interludes of buffoonery, which took place only now and then, seemed to provide an antidote that relieved the strenuous concentration we always employed in our rehearsing.

I remember an incident that occurred when the Chamber Music Players were playing to the Bradford Music Society. During the interval I accidentally jarred the scroll of my viola against a door and to my horror the sound-post inside the instrument fell down. Albert, who was a handy-man, came to the rescue and asked for a teaspoon and fork which were readily forthcoming. And believe it or not, he succeeded in erecting the fallen sound-post with these implements. Not only that but the position he got it into actually improved the tone of my viola! Apart from the piano quartet, I was often in partnership with Albert and have lost count of the innumerable performances we gave with orchestra of the Sinfonia Concertante of Mozart, every one of them a joy. What a natural-born violinist Sammons was. If only our country had done its duty by him and given him, in his early life, the facilities he deserved, he would I feel have been a very great international artist.

Between the years 1919 and 1921 I was busy making propaganda for the viola in concerts and lectures both in Britain and abroad. One was in Berlin where York Bowen and I gave a joint recital. Bowen was a prolific composer and a very efficient pianist, with whom I played a good deal. One of the works included in the programme was the C minor sonata for viola and piano, one of two sonatas he had written for me. It was a vivacious and light-hearted work and had a good reception from our German audience. The other part of the programme included piano works of Bowen's own composition and my contribution included Bach's unaccompanied Chaconne.

My activities, otherwise, especially in London, included broadcasts in which I railed most vehemently against the small so-called violas in use, to the exasperation of violin dealers; I did this whenever the opportunity offered – to such an extent that as a result of my tirades, to my satisfaction the dealers had difficulty in disposing of their small instruments which were neither violin nor viola.

In 1921 I received intimation from the Belgian Embassy in London that H.M. The King of the Belgians had bestowed upon me the decoration of Knight of the Order of the Crown, in recognition of my services to the Belgian cause during the war. I later learned from Ysaye, at a concert at the Beaux Arts in which I played, that the decoration also concerned my efforts in raising the status of the viola.

7

American Tours

In 1922 I went to America for the third time. This visit originated through my friendship with the famous American actress Mary Anderson who lived in Broadway, Worcestershire. In the course of one of the musical evenings at her house, I met John McCormack the Irish tenor. He heard me play and said: 'You must come out to the States, I will give you an introduction to my agent in New York.' (I had already sent my credentials to an agent with a view to solo appearances in America.)

My arrival in the United States began with a strange experience in the agent's office. I had not been in the room for two minutes when the telephone bell rang and, after a brief preliminary, I heard him say: 'Oh yes, I can sell you Tertis for so-and-so many dollars.' I felt like a captive on sale at a slave-market. But I soon realized this was the American way of quoting an artist's fee.

This was my first tour as a viola soloist. I gave a recital in New York and as a consequence was asked to play with the New York Symphony Orchestra under Walter Damrosch. I played the Dale Suite for viola and orchestra; then Damrosch insisted that my second item should be the unaccompanied Bach Chaconne which he had heard me play at my recital. His suggestion surprised me, for to have a large orchestra sitting listening and doing nothing for seventeen minutes must have been rather expensive! During this first tour I learnt how inspiring it was to play in America. The Americans are eagerly receptive, experienced in the arts, and discriminating. If your efforts satisfy them you may well pat yourself on the back. There was a great difference between the welcome I had there and the terrific opposition to my efforts that I encountered during my early years as a propagandist for the viola as a solo instrument in my own country – where I had to force my way through a dense labyrinth of antagonism and prejudice. I was literally treated as a nefarious interloper. One heard quite frequently in

England the comment: 'The viola was never meant to be a solo instrument.' Indeed they were ready to put me up against a wall and shoot my head off for my persistence in fighting for what was a just and righteous cause. Storms of abuse were my lot from anybody and everybody. But in America, my efforts to raise the status of the viola were welcomed immediately with open arms.

I joined forces for some of my recitals with Frances Alda of the Metropolitan Opera House, New York. We gave concerts in a vast number of cities throughout the United States and at one of the large halls we played in we entered the stage by an imitation door-way in the scenery. I pushed open this fictitious door and Miss Alda stepped forward to the footlights with me trailing behind (I usually played an obbligato to one of her songs), then she suddenly looked back at the aperture in the scenery by which we had entered and astonished me by addressing the audience with the words: 'It is usual for the gentleman to shut the door behind him when accompanied by a lady!' I immediately returned and shut the so-called door, apologizing to her and also to the audience for my seeming rudeness, and the concert went smoothly thereafter. As a matter of fact I think she was a little bit piqued by the amount of applause I received for my solo performances in these programmes and took this occasion to put me at a disadvantage, but the incident was like water off a duck's back as far as I was concerned and gave me and the audience something to smile about.

Among the delightful people I met on this tour was Mrs Frederick Sprague Coolidge, a great patroness of music. My particular recollection was of her very generous patronage of up-and-coming composers and talented instrumentalists. On one occasion she asked me to give a recital at her Berkeley, Mass. annual festival of chamber music. As far as I can remember, in one of these concerts I played a duet that I had written for two violas on a four-bar theme of Handel. This I subsequently dedicated to Mrs Coolidge; the manuscript is now in the Library of Congress. Also included in these Berkeley festivals was a Sextet for six violas by Benjamin Dale who wrote it for me at my instigation – a unique composition well worthy of repeated performances, but sadly neglected.

Mrs Coolidge was particularly friendly with my wife and generously asked her to be her guest on all the occasions that I played for her. Later she engaged me to give a few joint recitals in Milan, Pisa and Rome with Alfredo Casella, a most brilliant pianist, especially of modern music, and an excellent composer. She also invited me to play the Bach Chaconne at the American Academy in Rome. She made frequent visits to Europe commissioning composers such as Bartok, Martinu, Casella and very many others to write chamber music.

Her enthusiasm for music in general was unbounded and she was ever a most delightful hostess. I remember, in the very early days of our friendship, complaining to her about one particular difficulty concerning a few bars in one of the variations of the Bach Chaconne. I had worked at it for interminable hours, practising it thousands of times – all to no purpose, I could not conquer it. Her reply to that was: 'Forget about the innumerable times you have practised the difficulty, and attack it *as if for the first time*, keeping in your mind these two words: DON'T WEAKEN.' Two words that have influenced me to my benefit throughout my life, and incidentally, advice which enabled me, at long last, to master the recalcitrant passage in the Chaconne.

On my return trip home at the end of this tour of America Robert Mayer was a fellow passenger on the liner *Berangaria*, and in our talks together he bubbled with enthusiasm over some orchestral concerts he had attended of programmes for children, instituted and invented by Walter Damrosch. What a brilliant idea this was. As soon as Robert Mayer got back he put into operation the same idea in London. The movement, coupled with the B.B.C.'s ability to give music to the millions over the air, has borne fruit in the form of today's very much larger and more musically minded public for orchestral music. One has only to look round the well-filled halls at London's innumerable orchestral concerts to realize the importance of Sir Robert and Lady Mayer's work. Mayer persuaded Malcolm Sargent to help him in this scheme and he proved to be the life and soul of the Mayer Children's concerts in the early 1920s. Sargent's playing on the piano of extracts from the works to be performed, and his vivacious commentary, were the delight of all present – the young and the not so young. He would ask the principals of each section to demonstrate the qualities of their instruments in short passages from the works he was conducting, to enable the children to recognize the different instruments of the orchestra.

At one of these performances, which took place at the Central Hall, Westminster, Albert Sammons and I were invited by Mayer to play the Mozart Sinfonia Concertante. Her Majesty Queen Elizabeth the Queen Mother, then Duchess of York, attended with her two very young daughters, our present Queen and Princess Margaret, to all of whom Albert and I had the honour of being presented after the concert. These concerts and other musical activities of Sir Robert have gone on year after year, and now he is a fellow-nonagenarian of mine, still full of most astounding vitality. As a professional musician I am grateful for what he has done and is still doing for the good of music in our country.

A year later (1923–24) found me again on tour in America, and during this visit what seemed a miracle happened to me. I received an invitation from Fritz Kreisler to play the Mozart Sinfonia Concertante with him at one of his concerts at Carnegie Hall, New York. We had two rehearsals in his hotel apartment and he told me he had written two elaborate cadenzas for the first and second movements of the work, and when I tried them with him what magnificent ones they were, and jolly difficult. I had to learn them from memory in two days. During the second rehearsal Jacques Thibaud came in and listened to us, and he too was enraptured with the cadenzas. At the end of the rehearsal he turned to me and asked me if I would play the Concertante with him in Paris. Needless to say I felt very honoured and accepted with alacrity.

At the first performance of the Concertante at the Carnegie Hall with Kreisler, he insisted that I should go on to the platform before him, and when I demurred he said: 'You are my guest' – that was typical of his lovely nature. A similar example of his characteristic kindliness was, I remember, when he remarked to me, 'Whenever I attend recitals of my fellow artists, I never take notice of their faults – if any, I let them go in one ear and out of the other. But their good points I enjoy, and endeavour to grasp these and learn from them.' Indeed, never once did I hear him say a derogatory word concerning any artist.

After a second performance of the Concertante with Kreisler at Boston, he filled my cup to overflowing by suggesting that we should repeat it in London at the Albert Hall. It was like a dream, a wild impossible dream, come true. For twenty years I had been slavishly devoted to him; I revered him as the god of the violin; and now I was to play with him in my own London.

After my return to England I gave a recital at the Wigmore Hall. In America at that time there were no complimentary tickets to any concert, a rule that appealed to me very much, and I therefore instructed my agent in London to issue no complimentary tickets to

anyone for this recital. In the event only sixty people came! I
played the Bach Chaconne, Arnold Bax's sonata with the composer
at the piano, and a sonata by Martini arranged by Samuel Endicott,
given for the first time. Afterwards I addressed the audience, saying
I was sorry to see so many empty seats, but whilst my agent had
told me he could fill the hall by giving away free tickets, I preferred
to follow American practice and play to those who thought the
artist worthy of his hire.

A happy contrast to this occasion was the recital with Kreisler
at the Albert Hall. The piano accompanist was Charlton Keith who
invariably played with him in London. The hall was filled to
capacity, as it always was at a Kreisler concert. The press notices
were especially enthusiastic about Kreisler's wonderful cadenzas in
the Mozart Sinfonia Concertante. The *Daily Telegraph* reported
that the 'juxtaposition of sonorities' afforded by the cadenzas was
such 'that, with eyes averted, it was hard not to believe that one was
hearing a string quartet.' Under the headline '8,000 hear Kreisler –
a viola sister-voice', Richard Capell in the *Mail*, after paying
homage to Kreisler's incomparable qualities, went on most gratify-
ingly to describe the effect of the 'expressive, dark-toned viola':

> It was a different beauty, but a well-nigh equal one, and it was
> enchanting to hear the two singing, as it were, in affectionate
> mutual emulation. The violin would seem to be playfully
> challenging the viola to imitate its gay upward flight. The viola
> was not loth, and if it could not reproduce the other's brilliant
> accent its own turn would come after a time when the violin
> was demurely invited to match the viola's peculiar gravity of
> expression . . . The viola has in the past been the Cinderella of
> the string family, always overshadowed by violin and 'cello. It
> was very graceful of Mr Kreisler yesterday to help it to a new
> place. It was, perhaps, a turning point for the viola and for
> Mr Tertis, so long its splendidly gifted devotee.

Soon after this momentous event I played with Jacques Thibaud
in Paris. When I arrived in the artists' room there were a few friends
of Thibaud surrounding him but no one took the slightest notice of
me and I could see written on their faces, 'He's a Britisher, so I
expect his playing will be as cold as an icicle.' When we finished
the Concertante, however, they were all round me – I suppose

astonished that a member of the British race could possess so much warmth of expression in his playing.

Here I must comment on a matter about which I feel most strongly. The viola part of the Concertante is frequently played in E flat. I deprecate this transposition. It is much more effective in the key of D, as Mozart wrote it, with the four strings of the viola tuned up a semitone, and this is how it should be played. Throughout the whole work it is absolutely 'question and answer' between the solo violin and the solo viola, and tuning up the viola a semitone gives it a much more brilliant sound in keeping with the violin, while still retaining the characteristic C string sonority. The reason probably that deters most viola-players from playing the work in the original key (even if they have a good minimum-sized viola – 16¾ in. long) is that they shirk playing in the key of D, while the orchestra and violin soloist are playing in E flat. I can only say that this never bothered me in the slightest; moreover I can tell them that technically it is easier to play in D major. The fact of the matter is that many viola-players today play on under-sized instruments which have no semblance of C string sonority and if they were to tune their violas as Mozart directed, their C strings would make it sound *more than ever* as if they were playing on a piece of rope.

1924 was one of the earliest years of broadcasting. I remember the *Daily Express* sponsored a concert from 2.L.O., the then London station of the British Broadcasting Company. But it was Dame Nellie Melba who made the *first* entertainment broadcast over the air on 15 June 1920, transmitted from Chelmsford by the Marconi Company. In 1926 Dame Nellie Melba undertook a farewell tour of about twenty concerts in the provinces, at which she invited me to play solos. When I accepted, she wrote to me from Venice:

My dear Lionel, I am *dee*lighted that you will honour my farewell tour in England by playing for me. We must do the Mozart Aria. I wonder if you have a copy of my cadenza. I can't find mine (so like me). I return to England (for a few days) about the 17th September, so do ring me up, 5581 Mayfair, and we might have a little rehearsal and then you could give me the song.

Bless you,
Nellie Melba

The author as a Special Constable, 1914-18 (left); after the war (right)

In the garden of Hackwood, home of Lord Curzon, 1916. From left to right, standing: Eugène Ysaÿe, Albert Sammons, Emile Doehaerd, the author, Arthur Rubinstein. Seated: Princess Marie José of Belgium, later Queen of Italy (with governess), Baroness Ravensdale, daughter of Lord Curzon

'Twenties advertisement for the
author's Columbia records

Fritz Kreisler about the time
when the author first played
with him (1924)

After a rehearsal, with Albert Sammons (left) and Julius Harrison, permanent conductor of the Hastings Corporation Symphony Orchestra (centre) in the 1930s

Rehearsing with Solomon at H.M.V. Studios in the early 1930s

The author explaining a point in the design of the T.M. viola to violin-maker Arthur Richardson, 1938 (left); outside Buckingham Palace with Charles Lovett Gill after receiving the C.B.E., 1950 (right)

Bride and bridegroom play a duet after their wedding ceremony at St Sepulchre's, Holborn, 25 April 1959, with Sir William McKie at the organ

I remember before undertaking this tour I had occasion to consult my doctor about a troublesome cough. One of my vices was cigarette smoking – forty a day, beginning with a cigarette in the morning bath! My propensity, I confess, was never to do things by half. I revealed to my doctor how many cigarettes I smoked, which brought forth a stern rebuke followed by his assertion that it would not be long before I would be forced to cease appearing on the concert platform. This admonition brought me to my senses and I gave up smoking immediately, which was for me easier to accomplish than moderating myself in this pernicious habit. The cure which he suggested proved to be a success – the eating of boiled sweets from morning till night for a whole week! At the end of that period, during which I had frequent bouts of nausea, I completely rid myself of my slavery to the cigarette, and have never smoked since that week nearly fifty years ago.

During this farewell tour of Melba's, one of the arias she sang – which was included in every programme – was 'L'amerò, sarò costante' from Mozart's *Il Re Pastore*, for soprano and violin. (I adapted the violin obbligato for viola.) Her singing of this was divine: no more beautiful phrasing could be imagined. Melba, that great artist, was also a generous and delightful woman.

Her singing was unique. She seems to have received as a natural gift what others strive for with toil and tears and never quite attain. She sang with a perfectly lovely and perfectly even scale, and the effect was of simplicity and ease. I believe, as a matter of fact, she did not have to work much in her training-time. Her intonation was always faultless. No singer I have ever heard could trill as she did; the two notes of her trill were dead in tune, and the utmost brilliancy was maintained for its duration. The *Re Pastore* aria included an elaborate cadenza with florid decorations and a chromatic scale rising an octave to the B flat above the treble stave, with the viola accompanying chromatically a third below. Her singing of this scale was always a miracle of exactitude. All her life writers strove to describe the quality of her tone, but this was beyond words. It would, at the same time, be a lack of candour not to admit that Melba condescended at times to sing music unworthy of her voice and art.

My wife came to all the concerts of the tour and often accompanied Melba on walks. Once Melba said to her: 'People will remember me not by my singing but by what they eat!' Her term of endearment for my wife was 'little grey Mousie'. The last time Melba went to Australia she invited me to accompany her, to play at her concerts; but I loathed travelling and did not take advantage of her suggestion. On the voyage she contracted a serious illness and wrote a despairing letter to my wife, saying that something she had eaten on board must have been contaminated, and concluding with the words: '. . . hard if I should have to die now – I have such a lot to do.' She died in Australia in 1931.

Among orchestral concerts around this time that stand out in my memory are three in which the entire programme consisted of works for solo viola and orchestra. One was at the Wigmore Hall when I engaged a small orchestra and played Bloch's Viola Suite,* York Bowen's concerto and Dale's Romance and Finale, with Eugene Goossens conducting. Another was in Zürich at the Tonhalle, when the programme consisted of Mozart's Sinfonia Concertante, with the excellent leader of the orchestra as my partner, *Harold in Italy*, and Walton's concerto, Volkmar Andreae conducting. And the third was in Chicago, with the symphony orchestra under their splendid conductor Frederick Stock, himself a fine viola-player. On that occasion I played the unaccompanied Bach Chaconne as well as the Romance and Finale from the Dale Suite and the Walton concerto. (Strangely enough, very soon afterwards the B.B.C. invited me to play the Walton concerto again, this time with the B.B.C. Symphony Orchestra under Adrian Boult, in the same hall in Zürich.)

---

* Bloch originally composed his Suite for viola and piano. I gave the first performance of it with Harold Bauer at the Library of Congress in Washington. Bloch was present in the audience and some years later he arranged it for viola and orchestra.

8

Fruitful Years

On one of the most fortunate days in my life I made the acquaintance of the late Earl of Leicester. My first contact with Viscount Coke, as he then was, had been at the end of 1915 at one of his musical evenings at his London home, 4 Devonshire Street. The Chamber Music Players were invited to make music at this and several more of these evenings – Sammons and Murdoch managing to obtain leave from the Grenadier Guards.

Thomas Coke had just been invalided out of the Army, having served in France with his regiment the Scots Guards since the outbreak of the 1914 War. He had previously served in the Boer War in South Africa with the mounted infantry when he was nineteen years old. He also served in Italy in 1917. On my first visit to his London home with the Chamber Music Players I was intrigued with his musical knowledge and enthusiasm. He told me that as a boy he had to hide his violin under his bed, because his father disapproved, music not being considered at that time a fit occupation for one in his position.

I also visited him to make music at his lovely country home at Sowley, near Lymington, Hampshire, where he lived until 1941 when his father died and he inherited the family estate of Holkham in Norfolk and became Lord Leicester. There he organized several concerts in aid of war charities and served in the Home Guard.

In all I had the privilege of Lord Leicester's friendship for well over thirty years. Many are the hours I made music with him, and he was ever an inspiration to me. He was a born violinist and if, in his younger days, he had had the opportunities he ought to have been given, he would have been a magnificent player.

The marble hall at Holkham is one of the most beautiful in the world – a Roman basilica in form, and as wonderful acoustically as it is architecturally. One evening Lord Leicester said: 'Lionel, I should so like to hear the Chaconne in the hall – in the dark!' I never could refuse a request from him, so far as lay in my power. The lights were extinguished, and a singular experience was mine. I felt not that I was playing but that I was listening – listening in wonder to Bach's majestic music, as though I were not participating myself. The acoustics of the hall lent an incomparable sonority to the viola's tone.

Lord Leicester had a very extensive library of gramophone records and he invented some contraption – I don't know what it was – that was connected to the sound-board of his grand piano which improved the quality of tone of the records considerably.

On one of my visits to Holkham I met the Lady Fermoy, an amateur pianist and a pupil of Cortot. Many times I was to make music with her to my great enjoyment. She is one of those rare pianists who, seemingly by instinct, realize what you are about to do in the way of nuance and tempo almost before you do yourself; a born musician, and extraordinarily good at sight-reading.

Through the years my wife and I enjoyed many visits to Holkham and I have a vivid recollection of one occasion when I had become a septuagenarian. I complained to Lord Leicester that I was beginning to be old, and his reaction to this was quite staggering. He exploded, with extraordinary vehemence: 'Good gracious, Lionel, what stuff and nonsense, you are in the prime of life!' On a subsequent visit to him he reminded me of my complaint about Anno Domini and presented me with the following inspiring and beautiful poem:

> Age is a quality of mind –
> If you've left your dreams behind
> If hope is cold
> If you no longer look ahead
> If your ambitious fires are dead
> Then you are old.
>
> But if from life you take the best
> If in life you keep a zest
> If love you hold
> No matter how the years go by
> No matter how the birthdays fly
> You are not old.

I cannot say with absolute conviction that these delightful words were written by him, but I should not be surprised if it was his own composition. Be that as it may, whenever I feel a bit down in the mouth I read this poem and feel rejuvenated, refreshed and ready to face the vicissitudes and perplexities of life.

At the request of Sir John McEwen, Mackenzie's successor as Principal of the Royal Academy of Music, I undertook from 1924 to 1929 the direction of the ensemble classes there, as well as teaching the viola, and so once again became a Professor at the R.A.M. Among the quartets I coached was one consisting of Phyllis MacDonald, Adna Ryerson, Winifred Copperwheat and Joan Mulholland. These delightful and very young students accomplished the feat of performing all Haydn's eighty-four quartets, giving a concert a week in 1927–28 with three quartets in each programme, and never once from beginning to end did they miss a concert or fail to give a polished performance.

During these five years of chamber music coaching at the R.A.M. I would pick out term by term the best string players, with the purpose of constituting permanent teams. I chose for association those players I thought would match in as many ways as possible and might in time make acceptable string quartet combinations. One of these teams, to which I gave much time and care, cohered and in due course made a name for itself – the Griller Quartet. Another combination I thought would eventually make good consisted of Jean Pougnet, Hugo Rignold, Harry Berly and Douglas Cameron. It was a sorrow to me that they did not stick together. Pougnet and Cameron went their separate ways, and the Canadian Rignold won a place for himself as a conductor. But poor Harry Berly, alas, came to an untimely end. He was the best viola student I ever had and my hopes for him as a viola soloist were high in the extreme. I often think of him, he was a great loss.

I did not confine myself entirely to questions of ensemble, but also laid down the law on tone production. Invariably my viola was out of its case at these lessons and I demonstrated this practically. I must confess that I was often a real brute. I simply would not tolerate any faulty intonation. A former pupil whom I taught at a later period, Paul Cropper (now principal viola with the B.B.C. Northern Symphony Orchestra) recently reminded me of my words to him on one occasion, which may be taken as fairly typical of my attitude throughout my teaching life: 'If you can't play every note

in tune on that first page next time you come, I don't ever want to
see you again.' Another of my former pupils has told me that he
often rushed home after a lesson very near tears, because his intonation never satisfied me!

My ensemble classes took place in the concert hall of the Academy
(the Duke's Hall) so that any student as well as string players could
come and listen if they so wished. Unfortunately, absorption in the
teaching of so much chamber music playing began to take toll of the
hours due to my paramount object in life, and in 1929 I resigned
with regret and left again to concentrate upon solo work.

In the crowded years that followed, a memory I particularly
cherish is one of a performance (24 November 1931) of Strauss's
Don Quixote at Queen's Hall under Henry Wood, with Pau Casals
as the cellist and myself playing the solo viola part with him. In the
second part of the programme Casals played Haydn's concerto in D.
He was obviously in a nervous state just before going on to the platform and turned to me clasping both hands together, saying in a
piteous tone: 'Pray for me!' Needless to say the performance was
magnificent. Dear and great artist. One of the privileges of that
generation was to hear him in his prime. A grand soul was housed
in that small body – a body so small that it was always a wonder how
easily his left hand climbed over the range of the huge cello he
generally played upon. What supremely distinguished him was his
consummate musical understanding, but his technique itself was
fascinating, above all perhaps the cunning with which he would
change position on the long finger-board. A vice of some cellists is
an overdone portamento due no doubt, in some measure, to the
great distances between certain intervals owing to the length of the
finger-board. Casals's portamento was miraculously discreet, no
matter what the width of the interval.

One work, however, in the cellist's repertory, Brahms's first
sonata, the E minor, baffled even Casals in one respect. With all his
art he could not help making the cello growl and grumble in the
opening bars of the last movement; and the blame must be laid to
Brahms's charge. Brahms misjudged the medium when he wrote
the fugue at that low pitch. (This is one reason why I took it on myself to arrange the sonata for viola, which of course is an octave
higher, and therefore these incoherent growls were eliminated.) I
heard Casals play the work in 1945 at Chelsea Town Hall with
Gerald Moore as pianist. I happened to know that there had not

been time, on the eve of the concert, for more than one skip through the work. Yet the ensemble was excellent. But then Gerald Moore is astoundingly assimilative, as well as knowing the string repertory intimately. I had not seen Casals for years, and after the performance at Chelsea I went to greet and pay homage to the great master. His first words to me were: ' 'Ave you played for the sojers?'

I have made music with Gerald Moore countless times, and have always felt that he would be a collaborator with whom I should feel perfectly safe in playing a work in public without rehearsal. Among the frequent piano and viola recitals in which Gerald Moore and I were involved to our mutual satisfaction, one I distinctly remember occurred in Dublin during the 1939–45 War. Owing to the black-out the route we were obliged to take was via Manchester, staying at the Midland Hotel for the night and flying from there to Southern Ireland in the early morning, in a cockleshell of an aeroplane with its side windows covered over, and carrying only about eight passengers. I remember when we arrived in Manchester the city was in complete darkness with no taxicabs available. However, at the entrance to the station a newspaper van drew up and we asked the driver if by any chance he was going near the Midland Hotel, and if so, would he be good enough to cart us there with our luggage. His reply was immediate: 'Of course, I just have to get the news-papers from your train but it won't take long.' Meanwhile there was room for one in the cab of the vehicle and one inside. I elected to go with the driver and Gerald in the van with the newspapers.

The weather was extremely cold and I wore a fur-lined coat which had just been re-covered with a splendid and rather expensive cloth. After thanking the driver profusely for his kindness, we entered the hotel, the interior of which was brilliantly lit, and there I discovered to my utter dismay that the whole of the lower part of my fur coat was covered in what looked like a huge patch of very thick white paint or paste. Sitting next to the driver I had not noticed that between us was a pail containing this horrible liquid, and that a part of the bottom of my coat was in it. All the efforts of the valet service at the hotel could not remove this sticky mess from my coat, which was utterly ruined, but until I got home again I had perforce to wear it to keep warm and face the strange looks at me from passers-by. Eventually the whole of the outer cloth had to be renewed, so that this otherwise delightful professional engagement involved me in a distinct pecuniary loss.

9

The Elgar Viola Concerto

When once I was in conversation with Sir Edward Elgar I mentioned to him the innumerable objections I had met against my transcriptions. He exclaimed: 'What nonsense! What of the countless arrangements that the great masters themselves have made of their own works?' To follow up this remark of Elgar's I will give a few examples:

Bach rearranged his double violin concerto in D minor for keyboard, transposing it into C minor; he arranged two violin concertos for keyboard.

Beethoven, among his numerous transpositions, arranged his trio of two oboes and cor-anglais for two violins and viola. (Incidentally, I went one better than that; I arranged the work for THREE violas, and what is more I got it into print! True, there was a bit of blackmail involved in this astounding attainment. It came about in this way. A certain well-known London publisher made the proposal to me that I should transcribe what I would term the harassing, almost unending, mind-discouraging Sevcik violin exercises for viola (they are known in Germany as 'Hin und Zurück', which means 'There and back ad infinitum'). My mind immediately flashed back to my three-viola arrangement which I thought would never see the light of day, and without hesitation I replied: 'I will undertake the transposition of the Sevcik exercises providing you publish my three-viola arrangement of the Beethoven trio.' And that is how this marvellous achievement of a work for three violas got into print.)

Brahms arranged, among other of his works, his two clarinet sonatas for viola (or violin), and his quintet in F minor as a sonata for two pianos. By the way, to show the opinion *he* had of viola-players only as far back as 1895, Brahms – in his own arrangement of his E flat clarinet sonata where there is one passage which rises to C on the second leger line above the treble clef – evidently thought that whatever happens, anything that rises to this *dizzy height* must be avoided for the viola-player, and he therefore transposed some of the clarinet passages an octave below with the result that in one case he was obliged to leave the end of the phrase unresolved! (The note to end the phrase was non-existent on the viola, namely B flat, a tone below the C string.)

Schubert in 1824 wrote a sonata for piano and arpeggione, and later arranged it for piano and cello (or violin).

Schumann's three Romances for oboe and piano he afterwards arranged for violin or clarinet.

There are many other examples in which the great masters arranged their original works for various instruments.

To come back to Elgar. When I tried my hand at arranging his cello concerto for the viola he authorized me to direct that printed on the viola part in large letters should be the words: 'Arranged with the sanction of the composer.' The first time I heard this concerto, I had been struck by its suitability for the viola. How often I murmured to myself over the years – if only I could have a work from this great man's pen. Anyhow, here was the next best thing. In 1929 I undertook the transcription and then wrote to Sir Edward in fear and trepidation to tell him what I had done.

Elgar had for thirty years been the principal figure on the English musical scene. The *Enigma Variations* and *Gerontius* had made him a national hero; and the works that followed, the two oratorios, the two symphonies, the violin concerto and *Falstaff*, to name no others, had one and all stirred the public to an enthusiasm no other native music of such pretensions had ever known. To meet Elgar was immediately to be aware of a majestic personality. He was not easily approachable, and his speech with strangers was often laconic and rather forbidding. The clue to this lies in the fact that he was at heart a shy and sensitive man. Once the ice was broken he could be exquisitely charming. He was a man of surprisingly varied interests, and among his characteristics unknown to the outside world was a whimsical humour. He was also capable of expressing himself in biting words. I remember, early in the 1920s when 'bitonalism' was first heard of, his uttering an opinion hostile to the new dissonance in devastating terms.

To my request that he should hear me play his E minor cello concerto, I received, to my delight, a favourable reply, and it was arranged that George Reeves and I should go down to Stratford-on-Avon, where Elgar was then living, to give him a performance of it

6

with piano. Reeves, then one of the most accomplished accompanists in London, was later to leave us to make fame and fortune in America.

I had prepared a little plot to surprise Elgar. The slow movement of his cello concerto all lies within the viola's compass with the exception of one note. That is to say, it can all be played on the viola in the same pitch as the cello – all but a single B flat below the viola clef. How was this B flat to be tackled? I decided to do it by tuning my C string down to B flat for the purpose, and took Reeves into the secret. When we had finished the second movement, I engaged Sir Edward in conversation concerning certain passages I had slightly altered in the work, and told Reeves to tinkle on the piano during our conversation, thus enabling me to tune down my C string surreptitiously to the note below – B flat, in preparation for the slow movement, without Elgar being aware of what I was up to. The operation proceeded according to plan; and never shall I forget Elgar's looks of growing consternation as we approached the low B flat in this phrase:

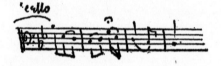

which in my version was written:

(C string tuned down to B flat)

I could see written on Elgar's face: 'Surely this fellow is not going to do this!'

When I played the low B flat he nearly sprang out of his chair with surprise and delight. I hastened to say that I had also written an alternative version of part of it an octave higher to avoid alteration of tuning, but his reply to this was: 'Oh, no, my dear boy – you must play it tuning the C down – it's grand!' I had let myself in for something, for the pause between the slow movement and the finale which follows it is extremely short, and the very few bars of orchestral introduction to the last movement are entirely off the key for tuning purposes. However, on the several occasions I have played the work I have always managed to tune my C string down successfully, though an alternative part has been published for those who would shirk tackling this.

To my pride and joy Elgar agreed to conduct the first public performance on 21 March 1930 at the Queen's Hall. I had been practising hard at the work and at the concert all seemed to be going well until, at about the twentieth bar of the finale, my A string broke! Everything, of course, stopped while I replaced the string (I had another in my pocket, so did not have to leave the platform), but it was as though a spell, as well as a string, had broken, and the finale, the last page of which contains the most heavenly and moving expressions of Elgar's genius, was besmirched, through no fault of my own, and for me there was a cloud over the rest of the evening. To celebrate the appearance of a viola concerto boasting the great name of Elgar I had arranged a supper party for a few of my close friends after the concert at the Ritz Hotel. But I was down in the mouth, and Elgar too seemed affected by what had happened. At table he had a little dig at me, saying: 'These affluent viola-players – they think nothing of arranging a royal banquet at the best hotel in London!' The papers next morning had more to say about the alacrity with which I had replaced the string than the important fact of a new viola concerto. However, I comfort myself in the knowledge that I have had the honour of being conducted in this lovely work by Elgar himself on several other occasions, which has helped me to wipe out the unfortunate happening at the first performance.

To go back to the dinner party: among my guests were three doctors of mine – Lord Horder the eminent general consulting physician, Irwin Moore, ear, throat and nose specialist, and Dr Charles Corbin, my very dear private doctor, all of whom kept me fighting fit. I was very fond of them all. Lord Horder to me was a

wonderful physician and his great characteristic was his common-
sense point of view in all his medical diagnoses. He was very keen on
music and I dare to say he was a fan of mine. I remember his asking
me if I would come and play after a dinner party which was being
held for the medical staff at his hospital (I think it was St Bartho-
lomew's). I recall an incident during my performance there. Evidently the dinner party must have been pretty convivial for one of the
medical men was considerably more than half seas over and persisted in muttering quite audibly while I was playing. I put up with
it for a short time until I could stand it no longer, then stopped and
addressed my audience: 'Ladies and Gentlemen, unless the semi-
conscious member of the medical fraternity is removed forthwith
I cannot proceed with any degree of concentration while his ridi-
culous interruptions persist' – and forthwith he was removed.

In 1933 at the Hereford Festival, Elgar again did me the honour
of conducting the viola arrangement of his cello concerto. The
performance went well and as we walked from the platform together
he whispered to me 'Good Boy!' – words which from him were high
praise indeed. I did once ask him whether there was a chance of an
original work for viola from his pen and he told me he had some
sketches somewhere, and he would look them up. He was not well
at Hereford but I had no notion of the dire disease that had seized
upon him and never for a moment dreamed that this would be the
last time he was to conduct. Alas, my hopes for an original work
from him were not to be realized, for in February 1934, a few months
later, this dear and wonderful man passed away. The works he has
given us, full of soul-stirring melodies, 'nobilmente' phrases and
wonderful orchestration, are something for which we should be
eternally grateful and crown this creative genius as an immortal.

Two other great misfortunes befell me shortly after this. Glazounov, whom I met in 1935, heard me at a concert and promised to
write a concerto for me. But the viola was to be smitten again, for this
fine composer died in March 1936. The other appalling loss I
suffered was a composition for viola that Ravel promised me. I
visited Ravel in Paris and played to him in his flat. It was winter-
time and the heat of the room was something I shall never forget.
It was like being in the hottest room of a Turkish bath. I played
Dale's Romance and Finale, with him at the piano. Ravel was
charming and complimentary, and at the end he promised to write a
work for viola. The score was to include a small orchestra and con-

cealed choir (bouches fermées). There was to be an alternative part for harmonium for occasions when a choir was not available. I went away rejoicing, but this great man died in Paris on 28 December 1937, a relatively short time after he had decided on the project. If only these three works, which fate willed the viola should miss by such a small margin, could have come into being, to join the splendid compositions for viola which we already possess from our own native composers, the solo viola library would have been much enhanced and would have raised still further the status of the viola as a solo instrument.

In 1929 I arranged Delius's second violin sonata for viola. The composer heard a gramophone recording of it, and sent me this letter, the contents of which overwhelmed me:

Grez-sur-Loing, 1/12/29

Dear Tertis, I have only just heard my 2nd Violin Sonata played by you for the 'Columbia'. It is marvellously beautiful, and I am overjoyed. I cannot imagine it better played. You have got *so* inside the music, and I never thought the viola could sound so lovely. What a great artist you are! The *Hassan Serenade* is also quite beautiful. . . . Please also thank Mr Reeves for his excellent collaboration.

Indeed, as far as I was concerned, George Reeves's splendid playing of the piano part helped the performance more than I can possibly say.

10

Heyday in the Thirties

Of the Hallé concerts at Manchester at which I played, one will always be memorable to me because of a performance of Berlioz's *Harold in Italy* conducted by Sir Hamilton Harty. I have often played this grand work, but Harty's interpretation excelled that of all the conductors I have known. In two places in particular the effects he achieved were incomparable. In the lovely Evening Prayer of the Pilgrims, with the answering intoning of the priests, Harty's expression was so vivid that one actually lived in the picture. Then in the final 'Orgy' those outstanding bars for trombones and tuba, with clarinets and bassoons, heralded by the violins' fortissimo shriek – Harty rendered the grandeur of these phrases of immense sound with an extraordinarily subtle rubato. What he produced out of these twenty-two bars was electrifying.

I have always felt that it is misleading to allude to *Harold in Italy* as a work for viola and orchestra. It is not. It is a work for *orchestra* and solo viola obbligato. This magnificent orchestral composition with its astonishingly advanced ideas of orchestration (considering the time it was written) and the lovely oft-repeated interwoven phrases for solo viola is a very precious possession in the viola library.

The première of this work was given in Paris at the Conservatoire in 1834, but it was not until fourteen years later that it was heard for the first time in England, and it is a great satisfaction to me to learn that on this occasion it was an Englishman who played the viola part – none other than Henry Hill, elder brother of the famous violin craftsman William E. Hill. Berlioz, in his book *Les Soirées de L'Orchestre*, refers to him as 'one of the foremost viola players in Europe'. He also mentions that Henry Hill was the possessor of an incomparable instrument, one made by the English violin-maker Barak Norman. This first performance took place at Drury Lane Theatre on 7 February 1848 under the auspices of Berlioz himself, in a programme of his own music. The programme was by today's standards decidedly lengthy, comprising the *Carnaval Romain* overture, first and second acts of *Faust*, finale of the *Symphonie Funèbre et Triomphale*, a 'romance' for soprano and items from *Benvenuto Cellini* and the Requiem besides *Harold in Italy*, which was described on the concert poster as a 'Symphony in Four Parts, with Solo on the Tenor'.

At Edinburgh in December 1932 I played in the first Scottish performance of Walton's viola concerto. Adrian Boult conducted. The applause at the end was long-sustained, and Boult amused me between recalls by whimsically suggesting that we should play the concerto all over again! I thought he was joking, and on again we went to the clamorous calls of encore ... encore. We returned to bow yet another time and to my amazement Boult calmly addressed the audience: 'I think it will be a help to us all if we play this work again. So I will ask your permission to beg the soloist and orchestra to repeat the concerto.' I will not try to describe how deep was my astonishment at what Adrian Boult expected us to do, but after the second performance I realized that conductor and orchestra had brought about a unique experience in the history of programme performance – a whole lengthy concerto as an *encore*. And nothing was thrown at us! The audience listened intently and vigorously applauded the second performance.

Outstanding among my continental excursions was a trip I made in February 1933 which included recitals in Rome, Milan and Pisa with Alfredo Casella. Casella was a brilliant pianist, his speciality being his performance of modern music for which he was world-famous. Included in the programmes were two sonatas for viola and piano by York Bowen, and my arrangement for viola of John Ireland's violin sonata in A minor. Casella played piano solos of his own composition and I also contributed the Bach Chaconne in our joint recitals. I enjoyed myself very much in this collaboration for his playing was magnificent.

From Italy I took leave of Casella and travelled to Berlin where I gave a recital, and I recall that Mrs Kreisler sat in the front row, and later in the concert Kreisler himself turned up and stood against the wall near the entrance to hear me play one piece – his arrangement of a fugue by Tartini for violin and piano which I always preferred to play on the viola unaccompanied, and did so on this occasion, because it was so complete in itself. He did not take his seat as he had to slip out to catch a night train. After the concert Mrs Kreisler paid me an overwhelming compliment by saying: 'I have never heard any string player whose tone quality was so like Fritz's.'

The next day I went to the Kreislers' home in Grünewald where Mrs Kreisler showed me their famous collection of antique china, which was unique. I seem to remember she told me that the British Museum had tried to induce them to part with this valuable assembly of china for exhibition with the offer of a fabulous sum which they rejected. Alas, I learned afterwards that during the Second World War the house was bombed and this priceless accumulation was smashed to smithereens.

After Berlin my journey took me to Paris with the sole object of visiting Delius. At the hotel, speaking no French I asked the porter to get me a taxi to take me to Grez-sur-Loing. I noticed that the driver of the taxi looked at me curiously, shrugged his shoulders and eventually said: 'Bien!' It was a horribly cold day, and snowing. After half an hour or so I became restless, but was unable to enquire how much further we had to go owing to my complete lack of linguistic talent. The taxi-driver pulled up at a petrol station to refill his tank, then on and on we drove. By this time I was in a state of complete collapse and frustration. Snow was falling heavily and I was shivering with cold. In vain I tried with violent gesticulation to find out how much longer the journey would be; my efforts were entirely fruitless. The driver was the most nonchalant and impassive human being I ever met.

It was at this juncture that a horrible thought suddenly struck me – should I have enough money to pay the fare for this long journey? I felt for my wallet, but to my utter dismay it was not in my pocket. I had left it at my hotel and had but a few coins with me. We were now travelling more slowly in deep snow, and demoralization set in. Eventually, Deo gratias, we arrived at Delius's house. Mrs Delius opened the door and I explained my predicament to her. She came to the rescue and lent me the necessary wherewithal to pay the taxi fare and I was told that their house was no less than forty-four miles from Paris! I should of course have gone by train. Once indoors my spirits revived. The house was beautifully warm and I began to thaw.

Never to be forgotten was the sight of poor Delius, so wan, so ill, in his invalid's chair. He was blind; and though I was prepared for a frail man, it was a shock to find him so near to being a living skeleton. Withal he was charming – though I was eventually told that this was not one of his better days. I had come to play to him my arrangement of his third violin sonata for viola. Before the music we sat down to a warming meal at a refectory table. There were just four of us, including Eric Fenby, pianist, composer and Delius's amanuensis. Fenby's devoted assistance to poor Delius was indeed a self-sacrificing, noble act. Delius was quite talkative – he wanted to hear all the news I had and amused us with anecdotes. The time came for our music-making, and the poor man swathed in rugs had to be carried to an upstairs music room by a brawny peasant who was the general factotum to the household.

Fenby played the piano part of the sonata splendidly and at the end of it Delius was quite happy about the arrangement I had made, said he had much enjoyed it and gave his consent to the publication of the work in this form. We played one or two other compositions for viola and piano which included the arrangement I had made for my instrument of his beautiful Serenade from *Hassan*, in which I repeated one of the lovely phrases an octave lower. He was so delighted with the idea that he burst out with: 'Why didn't I think of that – it is a great improvement!' To be with him was a most unforgettable experience for me. I returned to Paris by train, my thoughts full of sadness for the frail and awful condition in which I found this great genius. *His own fault (syphilis)*

When I returned to London I resolved to get into touch with Solomon with whom I had now and then made music. (His meteoric fame as a pianist at this time was already world-wide.) As a consequence of this meeting, we decided to establish ourselves as permanent sonata players. I had often thought of him since I first met him when he was a child prodigy. Extraordinary to relate, in close proximity of time I met yet another marvellous prodigy, John Barbirolli, who played the cello. One nine-and-a-half, the other ten-and-a-half, they were both to become world-famous musicians.

I had heard of Solomon as a prodigy from Mathilde Verne, a British pianist born in Southampton of German descent. She had been a pupil of Clara Schumann at Frankfurt, and taught and played much in London, organizing mid-day chamber music concerts and opening a school of pianoforte playing in 1909 at which Solomon, at a very early age, later on became a pupil. It must have been through Mathilde Verne's interest in chamber music that Solomon came to study the piano part of Dohnanyi's violin sonata in C sharp minor with her, for I played it with him at a public chamber music concert at Woodford in Epping Forest. His feet, at nine-and-a-half, barely reached the pedals, but he played quite astoundingly the very difficult piano part, not only technically but with mature musicianship.

Never shall I forget our association. One of the many concerts I played with him subsequently was a joint recital in the first month of the new concert hall in Broadcasting House on 29 October 1932. This was the third concert in the new hall. We played the Arnold Bax viola and piano sonata (one of the finest works Bax ever wrote) and the Brahms sonata in F minor. Anne Thursfield sang six songs of Bax. I remember we all remarked on the good acoustical properties of the new hall.

In 1933 Solomon and I gave a first performance of a magnificent sonata by Arthur Bliss for viola and piano, which he had written for me. This first hearing of a most valuable addition to the viola repertory was a private one, on 9 May at the Blisses' delightful home – East Heath Lodge, Hampstead Heath – to a very distinguished gathering of musicians, and I recall that William Walton turned the pages for us. It was a most exciting occasion, and we subsequently played the work many times in public.

Our rehearsals over the years included hours of striving to grasp the fullness of the composer's intentions, and we practised interminably to try to achieve perfect balance of tone. I shall live in enjoyment of those rehearsals to the end of my days. Solomon's control of the keyboard was absolute. He never made a show of his wonderful technique, so extraordinarily consistent in its accuracy. No matter who the composer was he captured his idiom and portrayed it with the deepest sincerity.

A story I gleefully chronicle that also happened in 1933 concerns my friend Ernest Newman, that wonderful music critic and writer, who at all times encouraged and championed my cause and whose memory I treasure. But on one occasion he wrote an article with which in some measure I did not agree. Anything however slightly derogatory to the viola immediately makes me see the red light and puts me on the war-path, and I at once wrote to him distinctly impolitely, not in any way mincing my words. The following letter was his reply.

Tadworth, Surrey, 10/11/33

Dear Mr Tertis,

Your letter was a double joy to me – in the first place because it is always a pleasure to hear from you, in the second place because it won me a bet. I had bet a friend, that the first letter I received on the subject of my article would be from you, taking me to task – sternly, of course, but still kindly – for what I had said about the viola. I want more readers like you, whom I can put to base uses of profit.

All you say is very interesting and, of course, quite true. But doesn't it rather support my case? *You* are thinking of the ideal viola that might be made. *I* was talking of the viola as the world has known it for the last hundred years. So we are not really in disagreement after all.

With kind regards, and my humble compliments to my ideal violist,

Yours sincerely

In 1934 I arranged Delius's double concerto (which he had written for violin and cello) for violin and viola. I was fortunate in having May Harrison as my partner. The work was written for and dedicated to her and her sister Beatrice, and she knew it inside out. This letter from Mrs Delius concerns the concerto:

I have just come back to Grez, and I want to tell you that May Harrison, altho' she at first thought it would offend her sister if she played the double concerto with you, has now found that her sister is not at all against it. As you said you had no violinist yet, I venture to suggest that you take her. She studied it one whole winter, under Delius's own guidance, and he always thought her playing very beautiful and musical. It would also save you no end of trouble with a new violinist.

The first performance of my version was with May Harrison on 14 November 1934, at the Queen's Hall with the B.B.C. Orchestra conducted by Adrian Boult, who was enthusiastic about the success of the arrangement. The work was well received by press and audience. It was a most valuable addition to the viola library but alas, it is rarely played.

Before this (on 18 March 1934) I had given the first performance of Gustav Holst's *Lyric Movement*, for viola and orchestra, which he wrote for me, again with Adrian Boult at the helm. The following letter came from Holst after the concert.

St Paul's Girls' School, Brook Green, Hammersmith, W.6

Dear Tertis, I send you my warmest thanks for the great treat you gave me and thousands of others on Sunday night. Your playing was perfect. I'm sorry I can't say the same about the piece itself. There is one bad bit of overscoring which makes me ask myself when am I going to learn the elements of my job. This shall be put right before the next performance.

If you have any critical suggestions I'd be glad to know them. (The bad bit is, of course, the 'squiggles' in four sharps.)
Yours ever, G.H.

In 1935 Dame Ethel Smyth asked me to edit her clever arrangement for viola, *Two French Folk-Melodies*. In this connection my wife and I went to visit her at her house near Woking. In her sitting-room we could not help being struck with the accumulation of incongruous objects. One such was a large and dilapidated kitchen-chair, with a huge rubber bed-ring upon it. Also present was an enormous, rough-haired, unkempt sheep-dog she introduced to us as her husband. I believe in course of time she had six of them! The years had not modified Ethel Smyth's well-known boisterousness and brusqueness. She was a woman of extraordinary strength of mind and directness of speech. I recall a public meeting of a musical society at which a controversial subject was debated. Ethel Smyth came last, and she totally eclipsed all the other speakers by the force and clear-headedness of her views. Often she was a trial to conductors. At a Queen's Hall rehearsal of one of her orchestral works, Henry Wood became irritated with her innumerable interruptions and directions. He finally exploded with wrath and said: 'Are *you* conducting this, or am *I*?' After this rebuke Ethel the fearsome, the one-time suffragette, subsided and became the acme of docility.

An episode of a like character occurred at Covent Garden during a rehearsal when Ethel was sitting in the auditorium listening to Thomas Beecham, who was conducting an excerpt from her opera

The Wreckers. She fussed Beecham to such an extent that he invited
her to take the stick and show exactly what she wanted. Without a
moment's hesitation, instead of taking the normal route to the
orchestral pit she vaulted over the barrier with skirts flying, to conduct the particular phrases as she wanted them.

Another 1935 concert that stands out in my memory was a B.B.C.
recital with Arthur Rubinstein in the concert hall at Broadcasting
House. Included in the programme was Arthur Bliss's sonata for
viola and piano. Rubinstein arrived from the Continent only on the
morning of the recital, and he had never seen Bliss's work. The
crossing from the Hook of Holland had been rough – he had twice
been thrown from his bunk. He turned up smiling all the same,
and the moment he arrived we had the rehearsal and the usual
balance-test in which he read the difficult piano score at sight. At the
recital that evening he gave an astounding performance, making
light of the intricacies and technical difficulties of the piano part, and
his interpretation musically was perfection.

Rubinstein's reading of the classics, in fact of any composer, is the
most satisfying and thrilling experience for the listener – something
to be wondered at. He is also unapproachable in his playing of
Spanish music. The bounding, joyous lilt he gives to such music fills
one with exhilaration. His equality of touch on all ten fingers is
remarkable, and he is the one pianist in the world for me who can
perform the miracle of making the piano sing in melodic phrases.
Indeed, more than once this god of the piano has brought tears to
my eyes by the marvellous way in which his fingers caress the keys
of this percussive instrument. His balance of tone between the right
hand and the left hand is always absolutely faultless. Another extraordinary feature of his playing is that however softly he touches the
keys one never misses hearing the note. As for his incredible technical ability – he plays 'second fiddle' to no one on this earth.

I seem to remember it was round about this time he was married
to Aniela Mlynarski, the charming daughter of the famous violinist,
conductor and pedagogue Emil Mlynarski, who was conductor of
the Warsaw Philharmonic Orchestra in 1901 and in 1904 Director
of the Conservatoire. Later he became conductor of the Scottish
Orchestra for five years. Among his compositions he wrote an opera,
a symphony and a violin concerto. Nela I am sure inherits her
musical sensitivity and discerning musicality from her father. She
was a great stimulus to her husband's career for she encouraged him

to practise hard and made sure that he was not distracted by anything or anybody.

At that particular B.B.C. concert I played Bach's Chaconne; and
a few days later I received a copy of a letter from the music critic of
the *Daily Mail*, Edwin Evans, which he had written to the Oxford
University Press:

> I heard Tertis play his transposition of the 'Chaconne', and I
> am in favour of its being published. Not many viola players will
> be equal to playing it as he does, but they will all want to have a
> stab at it. As it becomes known it ought to be the equivalent of
> the 'cordon bleu' among them. On the musical side it struck
> me, while listening, that in sonority it was a distinct improve-
> ment on the original, though I may be stoned for saying so!
> The chords and arpeggios spread across the strings gain much
> in dignity by starting from a deep foundation. Moreover, with
> violinists I have always been conscious of a certain occasional
> scratchiness, which they complacently regard as inevitable but
> which, for my ears, mars the effect. With the mellower tone of
> the viola this becomes negligible. I was on the qui-vive for it on
> Friday and it never bothered me.

Apropos of this performance I recollect that sometime in the
1920s Sir Walford Davies invited me to give a recital at the Aber-
ystwyth University where he was then Principal. I remember what
a lovely broadcasting voice he had and I have always been one of his
admirers; but on this occasion my feelings towards him, to say the
least of it, were not exactly kindly. Just before I was to give my performance of the Chaconne Sir Walford suddenly said to me: 'I
should like to say a few words to the audience about this great
masterpiece – I will only be one or two minutes.' But to my horror,
this 'one or two minutes' discourse developed into a lecture on the
work which lasted some twenty-two minutes! I will confess here
that throughout the course of my long life of performing in public,
I was always nervous before going on to the platform whether the
work I was to play was large or small – in fact I always felt as if I
were being prepared for the operating table! I paced up and down
in the artists' room not like the 'little lion' of my name but, as the
minutes passed, becoming more and more like an infuriated bull.
When at long last Sir Walford returned to the artists' room, I some-

how or other pulled myself together and proceeded on to the platform literally shaking from top to toe; but when I played my first
notes, nervousness as usual disappeared. I have often heard artists
say they are never nervous. Those that are worth their salt who say
this are telling a great big fib.

Another great pianist of the time was Sergei Rachmaninov, the
master of such rhythm, such dexterity, such wealth of tone, delicacy
and general artistry that he came *near* to concealing the mechanical
nature of the pianoforte. The only time I ever met him was at a
concert I gave for the then 'British Music Society'. When I came on
to the platform who should I see in the front row but Rachmaninov
himself, which nearly reduced me to palpitation of the heart, for my
contribution to the programme was two movements *only* from his
cello sonata. How I got through these two movements with the
composer present I do not know. However, at the end of the concert
I plucked up courage and went to him, abjectly apologizing for the
iniquity I had perpetrated in not playing the whole work, but I
frankly told him I did not care for the first and last movements. His
reply, to my surprise and relief, was: 'I quite agree with you – they
are weak movements, I never play them myself!'

In January 1936 I undertook a tour with Clifford Curzon under
the auspices of the British Council, which was to include Prague,
Budapest, Sofia, Cracow and Warsaw. I particularly enjoyed the
Budapest recital for the acoustic qualities of the chamber music
hall were inspiringly good. The sounds seemed wafted away with so
mellow a resonance, such clearness in pianissimo and without the
slightest echo in fortissimo. But let me tell the reader the following
astonishing facts: there were two massive stone pillars at the back
of the platform; and in the auditorium were quite a number of
similar pillars in the centre and at the sides. When we first saw them
at our morning rehearsal Clifford and I were filled with dread. How
could music possibly sound well with these obstructions? So much
for our knowledge of the mysteries of acoustics.

During our recital in the evening, while we were playing a Brahms
sonata, to our amazement not one but two cameramen with their
tripods calmly walked along the gangway in the auditorium and
proceeded to fix up their apparatus. Not only that, but during the
manipulation of their instruments of torture they also used their
flashlights – all this in the middle of a movement. I could see that
poor Clifford was very much upset, but personally I always made it a

rule of mine never to allow untoward incidents to disturb me when on the platform (short of the place being set on fire). I afterwards learned that this procedure was apparently normal at concerts in Hungary!

Our next concert was in Sofia. After playing Bach's Chaconne which came before the interval, I was in the artists' room when a huge man with the longest and widest black beard I have ever seen came in, made a bear-like spring at me, and hugging me, kissed me on both cheeks and completely enveloped me in his beard. It was a kindly meant way of congratulating me, but the sequel – at least I regarded it as such – was that next morning I awoke with a cold, and we had to catch a train to Rumania. As the journey progressed I got worse and worse, until on arrival at Bucharest I was running a pretty high temperature, and was convinced that my adventure with the black beard was the cause.

I was put to bed immediately and a doctor was sent for. We were due to play to Queen Marie of Rumania that evening, but alas, I had to forgo this honour and Clifford gallantly played solos instead, as he also did at the public concert. The doctor arrived and after he had prescribed for me, a little later, to my astonishment, along came an assistant, who brought a number of what looked like upturned glass egg-cups and fixed them all over my chest. I was eventually told that this was a cure for pneumonia – similar to the effect of leeches which were applied in the old days for most ills. I knew nobody in the hotel and Clifford had to leave me and finish the tour, giving piano recitals in the remaining cities Cracow and Warsaw. Fortunately for me there was a charming English woman resident in the hotel who was kindness itself. She took pity on me and nursed me through this very uncomfortable illness – a wonderful act of Samaritanism towards a complete stranger. At long last I returned home feeling disconsolate at having failed the British Council.

A Dark Cloud

There was another reason why I returned home depressed. In 1937 a cloud that had been looming for some considerable time darkened over me still further. Little by little I had had to cut down my repertory because of a physical affliction – public enemy number one, rheumatism. Fibrositis in the right arm had for some time gradually been depriving me of an essential of essentials – spiccato bowing, without which no string player has a right to perform in public. The malady was becoming acute and interfering very much with my playing capability, and by the end of 1936 I managed only with great difficulty to conceal the shortcomings of my bow arm. The fear haunted me that if I were to continue playing, I should deteriorate more and more and undo the years of struggle on behalf of the solo viola. I decided that the symphony concert at the Queen's Hall on 24 February 1937, at which the B.B.C. had invited me to play in celebration of my sixtieth birthday, should be my swan-song. On the evening of the day before the concert, I wrote a letter to Richard Capell, chief music critic of the *Daily Telegraph*, telling him of my decision and the reason for it, and asking if he could see his way to printing this 'obituary notice' of mine so that the situation could be made clear to my colleagues and the public. The following Saturday, after the B.B.C. concert, my letter appeared in the 'World of Music' column which Capell edited, alongside an article. 'It remains to add,' the article said, 'that absolutely no one who attended the concert on Wednesday had a suspicion of Mr Tertis's decision. On Thursday morning the *Daily Telegraph* said: "Viola playing of the kind we had from him last night has not been heard in this or any other country before." '

The part of the programme in which I joined consisted of Walton's viola concerto and Berlioz's *Harold in Italy*. As for my feelings when the concert was over, I will only say inadequately that grief and utter despondency prevailed; some sort of nerve storm overwhelmed me,

7

my distress was wellnigh unbearable and without staying to say a word of thanks to Ernest Ansermet who had conducted the B.B.C. Symphony Orchestra or anyone else, I collected my viola and other belongings as quickly as I could and fled from the hall. Not for a long time did I get over this upheaval in my life, but at last I pulled myself together and tried to plan an existence which might still be of some use, and to live with the realization that at sixty years of age, the prime of life, my work for the cause of the viola had come to an end.

For nearly thirty years my home had been at Belmont. I felt I could not go on living there, saturated as the house still seemed to be with the sound of the viola; and my wife agreed with me that we should find a roof elsewhere. So we left Belmont for good. We knew of Broadstairs as being a small peaceful seaside resort in Kent, and we resolved to try and find habitation there. We succeeded in renting a house on the front overlooking the sea and lived there for six months. I little knew then that years later I would have the privilege of meeting our future Prime Minister, Edward Heath, who reminded me at a luncheon in London that I had lived in his native town when he was a young man of about twenty years of age. It was my ill-fortune that I missed making his acquaintance during my short stay in Broadstairs.

A little later in 1937 I parted with my Montagnana viola, my beloved and most trusty servant. It was a heart-searching wrench for me to have to endure, but I had no further right to this glorious instrument. It went *con amore* to my pupil Bernard Shore whose devotion to the cause of the viola has always been a great satisfaction to me, and I am indebted to him for the vigour with which he preaches the merits of the viola as a solo instrument at his innumerable lectures all over England wherever and whenever he has the slightest opportunity, which he is still doing as I complete my autobiography in 1973.

I had bought this unique viola in Paris shortly after the First World War. It was my rule never to fail to visit the important violin dealers in the cities where I happened to be playing, and in Paris during this visit I found at the well-known dealers Maucotel & Deschamps an eighteenth-century Montagnana viola which eventually proved to possess a truly wonderful tone. I took a chance in buying it, for it was shown to me in an unplayable condition, without bridge, strings or fingerboard. I was informed that the firm was busy repairing a Stradivarius as well as other instruments, and that it would be some months before they would be able to put the Montagnana in order. In other words, I could take it or leave it. I was tremendously attracted by the fine craftsmanship, lovely wood and varnish. I could not decide there and then, and I remember walking up and down the Rue de Rome, where the violin shop was situated, with my wife for a good three hours, trying to make up my mind. Finally my wife, who always had more courage than I, persuaded me to take it. No case was available – it was such a large instrument, $17\frac{1}{8}$ inches – so my wife came to the rescue by wrapping it in her waterproof coat, and that is how it was taken across the English Channel. Incidentally we were not bothered by the Customs. This magnificent Montagnana, exceptionally fine in quality of sound and depth of C string tone, was of enormous assistance to my campaign for the viola during my possession of it from 1920 to 1937. I was always in terror lest one day somebody would abscond with it, and I thought of all sorts of expedients to preserve me from such a disaster. One such plan when on tour was to hide it under the bed in my hotel room. On one occasion, in my absent-mindedness, I forgot all about it and motored quite forty miles on my way to my next engagement before I remembered I had left it under the bed. Thank heaven it was still there when I got back to the hotel nearly a couple of hours later!

Another of my safeguards was a secret detachable plug I had fitted to the electrical system of my car, so that it could not be started, and I could leave my viola in the car with locked doors when making a short call feeling comfortable that the instrument was reasonably safe. On the very first day I had this fitted my wife and I had an appointment with our chiropodist at Sutton, Surrey, and after his tender attentions, into the car we got. I proceeded to start it up, but it refused to come to life. For an hour I tinkered, hands black and covered in grease, but it remained obdurate. It was a Wednesday afternoon, with all the local garage mechanics away for the half-day. Opposite the chiropodist's was a police station, and in desperation I implored them to help me. The constable who drove the police-van answered my request most politely and worked away at the car for a further half-hour, but all to no purpose. He then conceived the idea of bringing out the Black Maria, fixed a rope to our car and pulled us through the streets of Sutton hoping to bring it back to life in this way, but again without success. He finally towed us to a garage where we left it for attention the next day. My wife and I ignominiously returned home in a taxi. At three in the morning I woke with a start, sprang out of bed like a shot out of a gun and rushed to my waistcoat pocket. There I found my secret plug innocently reclining.

In May 1937, some three months after my retirement from the concert platform, I was deeply touched to receive a letter from my friends Albert Sammons, William Murdoch and Sir Robert Mayer informing me that a dinner in my honour was to be given on 13 June at Pagani's famous Restaurant in Great Portland Street, an establishment well known and patronized by the artistic fraternity far and wide. Among the many guests were Sir Hugh Allen, Sir Arnold Bax, Sir Thomas Beecham, Sir Adrian Boult, Antonio Brosa, Richard Capell, Arthur Catterall, Eric Coates, Harriet Cohen, B. J. Dale, Eric Fenby, Eugene Goossens, Beatrice Harrison, Julius Harrison, Lady Jowitt, Dr Stanley Marchant, Sir Robert Mayer, Baroness Ravensdale, Ernest Read, W. H. Reed, Felix Salmond, Sir Malcolm Sargent, Cyril Scott, Bernard Shore, Solomon, Maggie Teyte, Frank Thistleton, Ralph Vaughan Williams, and representatives of the *Morning Post*, the Press Association, the *Daily Telegraph* and *The Times*.

Sir Hugh Allen read telegrams from those unable to attend: Kreisler, Walton, Schnabel, Barbirolli and Szigeti. Among the letters I afterwards received was this from Pau Casals:

[Translation from the French]

Barcelona, 27 June 1937

My dear and much-admired colleague,

I am sending you these few lines belatedly to congratulate you on the tribute which has been made to you by your friends, colleagues and admirers. I should have liked to be with you on this occasion to express, along with them, the sentiments that we feel for you, for the man and the artist. Only your decision to retire from your public upsets us all because this represents an irreparable loss to our art. We all hope that this good-bye will not prevent your returning from time to time. Forgive the delay but I would ask you to take into account the great preoccupations that absorb us all here.

Your devoted, affectionate friend and colleague.

Pau Casals

I here give the content of some of the speeches as they were taken down at the time – for their entertainment value (the first two of them at least) rather than with any intention of blowing my own trumpet.

Dr Vaughan Williams referred to the news of Tertis's retirement, due to his alleged inability to play spiccato. 'I don't even know what spiccato is,' he added. He spoke of the letter he had written to Tertis, promising that all those who tried to write works for him would guarantee to include no spiccato bowing. He said that although one had to respect the decision of so great an artist, he was sure that Tertis's second best was good enough for us. He told the story of how, having written a few small pieces for Tertis, he invited him down to play them over. Unable to find an accompanist he had to play himself. As though this were not bad enough, they found that his miserable piano was half a tone flat. Tertis tuned down, set to work and after following the accompanist right through, apologized for his own shortcomings. The golden tones, passionate utterances and wonderful phrasing would always remain in the memory of those who had heard him, and even those who had not would live richer lives because Tertis had played, perhaps even before they were born. A beautiful thing, once created, remained with us for ever, in spite of the follies of all times. Had he played on a desert island it would still have been always with us. He recalled the legend of King Arthur; how before he died, he swung the sword Excalibur thrice round his head before throwing it into the lake, to show how it should be used. 'We know where Excalibur lies,' he continued, 'and how in the same legend Merlin prophesied that Arthur should come again to rule over his people. May this prove a true allegory!'

Sir Thomas Beecham then spoke of the highly emotional and perfectly justifiable speeches that had been made on Tertis's retirement. He wished to paint another picture of his recollections of Lionel, and to touch on another which had received less attention. He spoke as a conductor. It was impossible to realize what the viola section of an orchestra was like when he started as a very young man. Their reputation was even worse than that of horn-players! They were the despair of conductors, the

diversion of the audience and the perpetual exasperation of the
Press, or at least of that section of the Press which knew what a
viola was. This Cinderella branch of the orchestra was considered to be one of the necessary and unavoidable evils which
had to be endured. Then this worker of miracles appeared on
the scene. How he did it, no one knows; but the fact that the
whole balance of the modern orchestra was rectified was due
from A to Z to Tertis. He had heard the long and justified
praise bestowed on him as a virtuoso; but when the history of
music here and abroad came to be written, this saving of the
orchestra's 'distressed area' would be recognized as his greatest
achievement. This was an imperishable contribution, by means
of which he would be as well known as Queen Victoria, Glad-
stone, Casanova and any other historical figure. You cannot, he
said, discern anything of Tertis's personal life from the tranquil
façade of his face. He had been a rowdy uproarious young
bounder, unequalled in Chicago or Cincinnati. He recalled
their early exploits on the football field, in hotels and railway
stations and, in particular, one occasion when in company with
Waldo Warner and Warwick Evans he had left the train and
proceeded to uncouple the engine, to the subsequent amazement of the officials. The romantic side of his nature was a
closed book to the present generation. He had wandered all
over the world with his mysterious instrument, and knew every
little town between London and Odessa. He had even played
English music everywhere, but was still alive! And this was not
all. He had once received a compliment which any musician
might have envied. When he, in the company of Ethel Smyth,
met Tertis one day, the famous English composer, after having
stared at Tertis for some time, plucked at Beecham's sleeve
and said: 'That is the only man I have met in my life I should
like to have married.' When the time came to erect a monu-
ment to Tertis, he suggested that this remark should be
inscribed thereon as a tribute to his charming and popular
personality.

In such a state of nervousness had I been throughout the dinner
at the thought that I should have to make a speech, that I ate hardly
a morsel. I managed, however, to say what I wanted. Here are my
words as reported in the *Daily Telegraph*:

My advocacy of the viola was the result of accidental contact with the instrument about forty-four years ago, when I at once realized its attractions and its undeserved neglect. It was at that time the Ugly Duckling – barely tolerated – and however inadequate my efforts have been, I do take deep satisfaction in the fact that I was one of those who helped to rescue it from its invidious position. Of course this could not have been accomplished had it not been for our composers, who have provided the most extensive and the world's best library of solo viola music, for which viola-players will ever feel the most intense gratitude.

Now I should like to make an explanation concerning the discontinuance of my work. I want to take this opportunity to try and remove a little scepticism which I know exists with regard to the cause of my retirement. I ask you all to believe me when I tell you that my resolution did not come about without good reason and mature thought.

For some two years I have had to resort to subterfuge to cover up the deficiencies in my playing. My colleague, Albert Sammons, will bear me out how some eighteen months ago, in desperation, I sent him an S.O.S. and confessed to him the failing in my bowing technique which had come upon me. He tried all the tricks of the trade to overcome my difficulties, but without avail – and like the good friend he has ever been to me, he kept my secret.

The trouble rapidly reduced my repertory and the position became untenable. I ask you to accept this explanation of my action in retiring at the tender age of sixty. I had quite hoped I was good enough for another five years, but I am sure you will agree with me that having preached the Gospel of the Viola for so many years, it was time to give up when I realized I could not entirely practise what I had preached. I found myself unable to give the viola my complete powers, such as they were, and my course became very clear. I felt I would rather renounce my calling than bring to it a hampered service.

I do not allow myself any pity. Indeed the pity would have been if I had gone on and made a mess of things. I alone know how little I have done. But I shall permit myself the joy of looking upon tonight's gathering as the seal of recognition of the viola as a solo instrument.

However, my severance from the viola was not to be complete. First of all, I got to work on the ideas I strongly held of how to produce good tone quality in string playing, and wrote a treatise on it, *Beauty of Tone in String Playing*, which was published by the Oxford University Press (a revised and expanded version is included in the present volume). I also found myself doing more teaching than ever. I went to London from Broadstairs twice or three times a week. I had no viola, and gave lessons without an instrument in my hand, having promised myself I would not play again. But the deprivation I felt as a teacher, the predicament of not being able to demonstrate to my pupils, made me break my resolution. How could I come upon a viola? Any nondescript instrument would do. I went into nearby Margate one day, and in an old furniture shop I noticed a small fiddle which must have been a viola d'amore. Its tone was a wheeze, but its price was only £3! For a while it served my purpose. Later Eric Coates, my pupil of whom I have spoken on a previous page, lent me his instrument for a time for my pedagogical activities.

From the moment I decided to give up playing, my mind also found refuge in a project I had for many years wished to realize. This was to put into practical form my theories of a rightly designed viola, and the man to help me was Arthur Richardson whom I had met in Bideford some time in 1926. This violin craftsman of Crediton, Devon, attended a recital I gave in Bideford (I was playing on my 17⅛-inch Montagnana) and he came to see me in the artists' room to ask permission to make a template of my instrument. In the course of our conversation he appealed to me as a man whose artistic instinct was stronger than the commercial side of his craftsmanship, and I decided that he would be the fiddle-maker with whom I would collaborate in an endeavour to produce an ideal viola. My opportunity came at long last in 1937, for after ten months of exile I had more or less recovered from the shock of having to renounce playing the viola in public. My wife and I went to live in Bath to be nearer Crediton and our association began.

In the first instrument Richardson made, the thicknesses of the top of the back plate were at fault, and more than once he had the difficult task of unglueing the plates for alteration. He eventually found a method of inserting strips of newspaper round the edges where the glue was applied. This made it a simple matter to take the viola to pieces for rectification without injury. Indeed, the viola often arrived by post at my hotel in Bath with strips of the *Daily*

Telegraph sticking out like a frill round the fiddle between plate and ribs! While at Bath I drove to Crediton and back at least three times a week to be in close touch with him (a bit of a journey in one day) and gradually the quest for a satisfying viola came to fruition, with the eventual result that between 1937 and 1940 Richardson alone produced and sold nearly a hundred violas. The problems that faced us both I described in a paper I read at a demonstration concert at the Wigmore Hall on 4 December 1950, the text of which the reader will find at the end of this book.

A year or two after Richardson had made the first 'Tertis Model' viola I asked him to make a drawing of the design, but it was so poor that I would have nothing to do with it. Meanwhile an amateur fiddle-maker, Mr Charles Lovett Gill, a very eminent architect, got into touch with me and asked me to come to his office in Russell Square. I took my viola with me and he showed me a violin he had made which was excellent. He was most interested in my viola and wanted to make one – with the result that in due course he built seven Tertis Models, one of which was played at the demonstration concert at the Wigmore Hall. It was from him that I obtained a splendid diagram of the design of the 'T.M.' viola; also with his help I drew up a separate specification from scroll to tail-pin to go with the drawing, and I saw to it that all my measurements were absolutely accurate in the minutest detail.

These diagrams and specifications are to be found in many countries and I want now to place on record my indebtedness to Miss Seymour Whinyates, the indefatigable Director of Music of the British Council from 1943 until 1960. During the major part of this period she found time among her numerous strenuous duties to propagate and distribute the drawings and specifications of the T.M. viola to British Council officers in various parts of Europe, who in turn passed them on to the best craftsmen in their vicinity. Innumerable were the times that I gatecrashed her office in Davies Street to ask for her advice and help, and however busy she was, she was always ready to assist me in my campaign for the new design of viola. Her efforts through the British Council have meant much to me and I shall ever be grateful for her interest in my cause.

While I was living in Bath I saw that Kreisler was giving a recital at the Colston Hall, Bristol and it was with great happiness that I went to hear him – without his knowledge. As usual I was enthralled, and in the interval I sought him out, eager to have a word with him. When I entered the artists' room he was in the act of raising a cup of coffee to his lips. When he saw me he stopped, put it down, and before I could utter a word, exploded with wrath at my having thrown up the sponge. He would not listen to a word about my afflicted arm but insisted that I could get round the handicap somehow. He said: 'You must come and have supper with me and we will talk things over.' Seeing that I had a bundle of papers in my hand he said: 'What have you got there?' I told him it was the proofs of my treatise *Beauty of Tone in String Playing*. After the recital we drove to the hotel and he said: 'I should like to read your article on tone production – can you leave it with me for one or two days and I will post it back to you.' It duly arrived with the most lovely appreciation of my essay which he said I could use as a foreword if I felt so inclined; needless to say I jumped at it.

12

Collaboration with Beecham, 1938/9

On 28 March 1938 I was the guest of honour of the London Musicians' Club. I took the opportunity to express my views on the conditions under which our orchestras worked at that time. My criticism was that their weekly schedule was far too exhausting, resulting in mass-production and consequent deterioration in quality of performance. The next day the *Daily Telegraph* quoted my remarks, which brought forth from Beecham a rather tart and of course witty reply. Our exchanges on the matter went on in this newspaper for some considerable time and relations at the end of it were somewhat strained between us. It was some months before I met Sir Thomas again and the occasion was a sudden invitation from him to lunch which I very promptly accepted, and he greeted me with: 'Hello – what fun we had in the *Daily Telegraph*!'

Some time later he asked me if I would attend his rehearsals at Covent Garden and also his concerts during the year, to help correct the balance of tone, and to edit his string parts. I fell in with his wishes on condition that after a trial he was confident that I was proving of some help to him. I set to work, concentrating on achieving unanimity in fingering and phrasing – an important factor in expressive string playing, especially in a body of players performing the same melodic phrase. One day when I was carrying out my duties at an orchestral rehearsal at the Albert Hall, with my beloved Kreisler playing Tchaikovsky's concerto, I suggested that at a certain point in the score the orchestra had been too loud, and that Kreisler should play up. Immediately Kreisler turned to me and said: 'I agree,' and then quite meekly: 'I will try – I will do my best.'

At Beecham's season of opera at Covent Garden I continued to edit the parts, etc. and criticize the balance of tone. In my collaboration with Beecham I had all along been dissatisfied with the tone quality of the viola section and one day approached him to suggest my taking on the members of the section individually (providing they were willing) and giving them hints on tone production. Beecham's reply was characteristic – 'My dear boy, do what you like with them,' and then he bellowed – '*Boil them if you like! !*' History does not relate that I exactly did that but I went about it in my own way and the result was satisfactory.

Here are a few more of Beecham's quick-witted quips that I witnessed personally, and they prove that whatever you said or did, Beecham always had a reply which went one better. In the last thirty years of his life, wherever he went and whatever programme he played the hall was always full, even when on one occasion in London the programme was entirely made up of weak sentimental French music. I attended many of his concerts and I am certain he had his tongue in his cheek when he arranged this one, to show that whatever he played the hall would be full. I went to see him in the artists' room as I usually did at the end of his concerts and remonstrated with him for having given a *whole* programme of second-rate French music. Quick as a flash as usual, he replied: 'Well – there's nothing *illegal* about that!'

Beecham was very often unpredictable in his actions. The following episode is I believe well known, but has been inaccurately quoted. It occurred while I was walking up Regent Street with him after a rehearsal. It was a warm summer's day, and for some unearthly reason he was carrying an overcoat. Suddenly realizing that it was rather cumbersome, what should he do but hail a taxi (at a time when taxis were allowed to crawl along the side of the pavement), open the door, throw his coat on the seat, slam the door to and then say in the grand manner, in stentorian tones: 'Follow me, my man.' And there we were the two of us walking, engaged in conversation, the whole length of Regent Street with the taxi crawling along beside us, the driver wreathed in smiles. When we reached Oxford Circus he paid the taxi man and told him to take his coat and deliver it to his home in Grove End Road.

On another occasion I went to a rehearsal in the morning for a concert he was giving that same evening, and after he had been through a work by Berlioz in which the viola section had an important melody to play, I complained to him that the violas in this solo part had sounded particularly dull. He said nothing but I think this remark must have piqued him, for at night it was astonishing how he revolutionized their playing of the passage. The melody was really expressive. Afterwards in the artists' room I blurted out to him – 'What a metamorphosis you accomplished in the viola section's anaemic playing this morning! I believe you could draw blood from stone.' Like lightning he replied: 'Well, that's better than drawing stone from blood!'

Beecham usually turned up at rehearsals looking suave and amenable, but at the first rehearsal for one production of *Don Giovanni* he came looking morose, with stiff upper lip and monosyllabic. I knew that a storm was brewing and sure enough it happened in the early part of the opera, where Don Giovanni sings a duet with the female he tries to seduce and the father of the girl rushes on with sword in hand, a duel with Don Giovanni ensues, and the father falls mortally wounded and with his last breath joins in the singing.

Sir Thomas was dissatisfied with the vocal efforts of Don Giovanni and the girl and asked them to go back and correct some faulty rendering that had occurred before the duel. The singers, perhaps nervous as a result of Beecham's demeanour, failed to find the place quickly enough in the score and Beecham became more and more exasperated and brimful of bellicosity. With arms raised to Don Giovanni and the girl to recommence he suddenly turned round to find the father still lying dead on the stage, oblivious of the fact that he was wanted to go over the scene again before the duel. Came the inevitable explosion from Beecham: on seeing the 'body' he literally yelled at the top of his voice, 'GET UP, CORPSE!!' There was a roar of laughter from the orchestra.

At another rehearsal at the Queen's Hall, Beecham invited a well-known foreign conductor to attend it, and asked me to find him a seat in the balcony. During the rehearsal Beecham played one item in the programme from beginning to end without stopping, and conducted it sitting down on the chair on the rostrum. At the conclusion of this performance he turned round and shouted to his fellow-conductor in the balcony – 'How's that?' The reply came, 'Very good.' But Beecham, evidently thinking this scant praise, bellowed, 'What? *Only very good?!*' The orchestra chuckled with merriment. Beecham turned round to them and said something else which brought forth a roar of laughter – heaven knows what it was!

Another incident I remember occurred at a concert. He was conducting, when out of the corner of his eye he must have caught sight of a woman in the front row who was calmly knitting. He stopped the orchestra, put his baton on his music stand, turned round, glared at the culprit and in slow measured tones said: 'When the lady in the

front row has finished her knitting, we will proceed with the concert.'
After which he began the work again from the beginning.

During my association with Beecham doing the 'balancing trick'
for him, there was one occasion at his flat in Hampstead when I ventured to rebuke him for setting a bad example to the orchestra by
sometimes turning up late for rehearsals. I also spoke to him about
his patent leather shoes which squeaked horribly during his stately
gait to and from the rostrum. His flat was on the top floor overlooking Hampstead Heath and I fully expected him to throw me out of
the window for my temerity, but strangely enough he was positively
meek and in a quiet voice said: 'I see the force of your remarks.'

It was a great privilege and a most enjoyable experience to be so
closely associated – almost daily for a year or more – with Sir
Thomas, that extraordinary man of genius.

13

Return to the Concert Platform –
and America

The 1914 War had until the last moment seemed incredible to those brought up under nineteenth-century liberalism. Yet more incredible would it have seemed that a second horror would be our lot within less than a generation. In a heavy air, very different from that of 1914, came 1939. One dare not peer into the future. I resumed practice, and found to my gratification that my arm had benefited from the two years' rest, and this amelioration encouraged me to look round and see if I could be of some use. Nothing occurred to me except to try and play the viola again for charitable purposes. Thus it was that I went back on my 1937 resolution. As a preliminary, I returned to the platform to give two recitals with William Murdoch in November 1939, playing on a T.M. viola made by Arthur Richardson – the first time this English viola had been heard in public. I also resumed broadcasting. Among the letters I received was one from 'Uncle Tobs' (Tobias Matthay, the famous pianoforte pedagogue). 'My dear Lionel,' he wrote. 'We heard you over the wireless the other day. It was as great as ever. And it was a great happiness to hear you again. The new instrument came through most effectively, too.' I also took up teaching again – this time at the Royal College of Music, joining the staff there a few days after the Battle of Britain had been won.

In 1940 I gave five recitals in different cathedrals for war charities: with the organist Percy Hull at Hereford Cathedral for the Bomber Fund (the collection, more than £100, included a gold watch and bangle), with Herbert Sumsion at Gloucester Cathedral for Gloucestershire charities, the third at Winchester with Harold Rhodes for the homeless at Southampton, the fourth at Exeter with Alfred Wilcock for the Lord Mayor of London's Distress Fund, and the fifth at York Minster with the organist Sir Edward Bairstow.

Albert Sammons and I were asked to play at a party in the home of Lady Colefax in Westminster. Lady Colefax was the wife of Sir Arthur Colefax, a brilliant lawyer, and was well known as a wonderful hostess in London, having frequent gatherings of musicians, painters and writers at her beautiful home in the vicinity of the Houses of Parliament. It was arranged that we were to start our programme with my variations on a theme of Handel for unaccompanied violin and viola. We had no sooner taken our instruments out of their cases when we heard the distant sound of the siren.

We both hurriedly decided (sotto voce) to ignore all marks of expression, repeat every variation and play double forte the whole time. This device effectively reduced the noise of the falling bombs to a minimum. Among the guests were Somerset Maugham and Ivor Novello who we could see had twigged what we were up to and thoroughly enjoyed our unmusical performance. By the time we had finished our protracted playing of the duet, we found to our relief that the raid was over, and Ivor Novello begged me to put on my mute and bring calm after the storm by playing the Serenade from *Hassan* by Delius which he loved.

I reached the age of sixty-five at the end of 1941, and the B.B.C. invited me to broadcast in celebration of my birthday. The B.B.C. broadcast concerts in the middle of the night at Evesham in Worcestershire in 1942, and I remember playing the Bliss viola sonata, which he wrote for me, at about three in the morning when my colleague Frederick Riddle was broadcasting in another studio. When I finished playing the work he burst into the studio and his first words were: 'How the devil do you get up to that last bar in the third movement?' (entitled 'Furiante', in which somehow my left hand at the end of a violent passage reached top E in the treble clef perilously close to the bridge – here the reader may remember the unfortunate experience of Hans Wessely at a concert, which I have already related). My reply was: 'The Lord only knows.' Of course Bliss wrote a simplified 'Ossia' for those last bars of difficult passage work.

I do remember that when I was confronted with passages high up in the vicinity of the bridge, I would don a very heavy, voluminous, moth-eaten fur coat while practising at home, which made these dizzy heights much more difficult to reach, so that when I had occasion to perform them in public, it felt much easier to accomplish when I was clad in an ordinary thin jacket.

It was also in 1942 that I made up my mind as to how best to quash a delusion that had been in my thoughts for a number of years, namely that varnish is one of the principal factors in giving fine quality of tone to a string instrument. It is not. The purpose of varnish, i.e. *good* varnish *properly* applied, lies in preserving the wood and enhancing the look of it. I decided that a good opportunity to disprove the fallacy would be a concert in August of that year at which I was to appear as solo violist at the Albert Hall, Sir Adrian Boult conducting (I think it was a Promenade Concert). I shall never forget the look of consternation on the faces of many of my colleagues in the orchestra when I appeared on the platform at the morning rehearsal with a naked viola – that is to say unvarnished, 'in the white'. When they realized what it was that I put up to my chin, how shall I describe their reaction? – they let out a terrific war whoop! . . . However, we settled down to the rehearsal, and moreover I played on this instrument at the evening concert. The consensus of opinion was that the tone quality of the instrument was all that could be desired.

Half-way through the Second World War my dear wife was torn from me – suffering from grievous illnesses. One of the nursing homes she entered was in Sutton, a mile or so from Carshalton Beeches in Surrey where we then lived. I could not stand the anxiety of her being in the vicinity of the unrelenting and frightful bombing, and resolved to try and find another nursing home deep in the country. I thought of Droitwich which I knew, but I went there without success. Eventually after much searching I found myself in Malvern where I succeeded in obtaining a room for her in a comfortable nursing home. Malvern was considered to be a pretty safe refuge in the War.

I obtained a lodging for myself quite close to the home which was of some comfort to me in my anxiety for my wife. During my stay I gave a recital there in aid of the hospital. It was a fortunate day for me, for among the audience was a Miss Jane Parke – whom I later found to be a fine pianist and instinctive musician. She was introduced to me after the recital and through her I became acquainted with Miss Winifred Barrows, one of the ablest and most delightful of women. She was headmistress of Lawnside, a famous girls' school in Malvern. Innumerable are the successes of her Lawnsidians. The arts played a great part in the life of the school. In later pages I speak again of Miss Barrows and Miss Parke, two of my dearest friends.

8

The War was still raging when my wife was able to leave the nursing home in Malvern and we found a small delightful cottage at Hereford, in the vicinity of which lived Sir Percy Hull, organist of Hereford Cathedral, whom I knew well. Not only that, but extraordinary to relate, my pupil Harry Danks was stationed there in the official capacity of sergeant in the Army and paid me a surprise visit much to my pleasure. He had been a pupil of mine since 1935 and continued after the War. He later won for himself an enviable position in the music world by becoming leader of the viola section in the B.B.C. Symphony Orchestra – a post he still holds as I write this in 1973. He has always had the solo viola much at heart and has demonstrated this at every opportunity.

During our stay in Hereford, I of course carried on with my London and provincial engagements. One such was an evening concert for a war charity at the Dorchester Hotel. Midway through this concert the sirens blared out and very soon afterwards the V-bombs began to fall in close proximity to the hotel. I remember the entrance doors were draped with very heavy curtains and the concussion of the bombs blew them wildly about – indeed the bombs were falling so close that we had to discontinue the concert. Suddenly to our amazement quite a dozen young women burst into the hotel with blackened faces. We discovered they were Wrens from a nearby hostel, and had evidently suffered a very narrow escape. At this juncture all of us – audience, performers and everybody else – were ordered to go down into the basement kitchens. When the siren eventually gave the All Clear, we thankfully returned and completed our concert programme.

I had been invited by one of the directors to stay the night at the hotel and I shall never forget the scene that confronted me early next morning when I left. Most of Park Lane, nearly to Marble Arch, was strewn with broken glass and when I eventually reached Paddington I found that part of the station had also been bombed. As a consequence it was very many hours before the train left, and a long and tedious journey home to Hereford.

In January 1940 I had received a letter from Sir Hamilton Harty in answer to one I had written to him, informing him that I had the idea of arranging Mozart's clarinet concerto for viola. He wrote: 'I am interested about the viola concerto. It ought to make a good piece for Viola. Good luck to it. I think you might suggest a few possible cuts especially in the last movement. It's rather long.' As a result of this encouragement I set to work at the arrangement and played it for the first time at a Three Choirs Festival at Hereford in 1946. That the prejudice against arrangements still existed was evident from the fact that most of the daily papers absolutely ignored this first performance on the viola, except one – the *Daily Mail*, which came out with a prominent notice under a huge headline: 'MOZART KNEW BEST.' It was a long review in which the word viola was mentioned innumerable times. I received a chiding in it good and proper for my 'effrontery' in daring to make this arrangement. The notice was written by Ralph Hill.

Two or three days later I was invited by Ferrucio Bonavia of the *Daily Telegraph* to a Press Club luncheon, and whom should I meet but Ralph Hill. He came up to me and greeted me with this jocose outburst – 'I suppose you'll be having me up for slander.' To which I replied: 'On the contrary, I am grateful beyond words for the publicity you have given the viola, moreover I don't at *all* mind being "second best to Mozart"!'

Then Bonavia coolly informed me, to my utter amazement and nerve-shattering horror, that I was to be guest of honour in place of somebody who had defaulted. To say the least of it I was truly taken aback for I realized this entailed an on-the-spot speech from me. During the course of the excellent lunch (for which under the circumstances I lost most of my appetite) I formulated more or less on what lines it would be and I began, 'Gentlemen, I feel like the lamb in the lion's den! But I say to you – I am an obstinate customer. For the last twenty years or so I have hurled vituperations at the press for their audacity in upbraiding me for my so-called crime of making arrangements from the classics, etc. for the solo viola. Moreover I am impervious to pin-pricks and the more you go for me, the more I shall do it . . .' This last remark produced a loud expression of merriment. I was magnanimous enough not to mention Ralph Hill's name, but told my audience that only three days previously I had received from one of their illustrious members what he evidently thought would be a damper on any further manifestations of my nefarious propensity for making arrangements. Instead, I told them, his tirade had been one of the finest notices I had ever received from the publicity point of view.

In 1946 I was awarded, by the Worshipful Company of Musicians, the Cobbett gold medal for services to chamber music. The next happening of importance was a recital I gave at the Royal College of Music with Lady Fermoy and Max Rostal in 1949, for the purpose of instituting prizes for viola compositions there. I was able to gather some £400. The result of the first competition was that not only were the works submitted of mediocre quality, but hardly a note was written for the C string! Which after all is the characteristic and satisfying sonority of the viola. As a consequence I changed the object of the competition and devoted the funds towards an annual prize of a Tertis Model viola for the most accomplished viola student in the College, until the wherewithal petered out.

On 21 August 1949 I suffered a terrible shock and deep grief when Thomas William Coke, fourth Earl of Leicester died at the early age of sixty-nine. It was my privilege to play a melody he had loved at the funeral service at Holkham Church, and as I played I felt his spirit near. His memory will never fade. His devotion to music was inspiring. He was the most lovable of men, and I shall ever feel the loss of his friendship.

In the 1950 New Year honours, King George VI graciously appointed me Commander of the British Empire, 'for services to music, particularly in relation to the viola'. Sir George Dyson, Director of the Royal College of Music, told me how delighted he was, and said he believed I was the first string instrumentalist to be so decorated. My wife was in a nursing home at the time and unfortunately for me, could not attend the ceremony. I therefore invited my friend Charles Lovett Gill to accompany me to Buckingham Palace. While we were having our photographs taken outside the Palace gates, he remarked that he had once been concerned with a fellow architect, Albert Richardson, in alterations to the Throne Room in Buckingham Palace, and I have since obtained the story from one who has worked for many years in the firm of C. Lovett Gill. Richardson and Lovett Gill, who must then have been in his early twenties, redesigned the interior of the Throne Room around 1903, working for the architect F. T. Verity. In subsequent years Lovett Gill was fond of describing how much the two young architects had enjoyed themselves doing their survey at the Palace, and how Richardson had sat in one of the thrones and 'knighted' Charles with a five-foot measuring rod. Strange that, in the end, it was Richardson who received the accolade.

In October 1950 Mr Frank Howes, then chief music critic of *The*

Times, wrote to me in his capacity as Chairman of the Musicians' Benevolent Fund, informing me that I was to receive the Kreisler Award of Merit – an honour that will ever be a source of intense gratification and pride to me.

On 4 December 1950 I gave a demonstration concert of the Tertis Model viola. Before the demonstration I read an address on the design of the T.M. viola (the substance of my speech will be found at the end of this book). I purposely did not play in this programme for I wanted as many different professional players as possible to perform on the instrument. Seven T.M. violas were used and in the Brahms sonata William Primrose played on four different violas for each of the four movements to show how easily one could change from one instrument to another – all of them being of standard size.

This brings to my mind that some years previously at a concert in Paris with the Lamoureux Orchestra, Beecham conducting, Primrose, then a most brilliant violinist, joined with me in a performance of the Mozart Sinfonia Concertante. At the end of the concert in the artists' room Primrose suddenly said to me: 'I am a disciple of yours from henceforth', and he immediately gave up the violin to become the world-famous viola soloist who has done so much to keep the flag flying for the viola as a solo instrument.

The year 1950, alas, was fated to end with a terrible calamity, for my wife became very seriously ill and from thence onward my place was with her and not with my work for the viola. Six times since 1944 she had been torn from me to enter nursing homes, and no human thought can portray the grief I suffered when, in the waning of 1951, she was parted from me never more to return. Words cannot describe her devotion to me and her never-failing help in my efforts for the cause of the viola.

Early in the winter of 1952 I had to undergo a serious operation, and through Providence, and the skill of my surgeons, my doctor and the devoted women who nursed me in hospital, I was soon well enough to take advantage of the good offices of the Musicians' Benevolent Fund through their secretary Frank Thistleton, who had been a close friend of mine for very many years. He took me to their convalescent home at Westgate-on-Sea where I received such extraordinary kindness that in a comparatively short period of time I made a complete recovery – so much so that in July I was well enough to take part in the King's Lynn Festival which I much enjoyed. While I was there it was my good fortune and a great honour to be called upon to play to the Queen Mother and Princess Margaret during morning service at Sandringham church on the Sunday of the Festival week. After the service Her Majesty asked to see my viola and her discerning interest in the design of the Tertis Model instrument was a joy to experience.

At the end of 1952 I left my home in Surrey to stay with my niece and nephew, Brigadier and Mrs Shaw who lived at Whitchurch near Tavistock in Devon. Their charming house was right on the edge of Dartmoor and I remember that I rarely missed a daily walk of about a mile and a half across the moor to a most picturesque little bridge over a rivulet which rejoiced in the name of 'Penny-cum-Quick'. Their sheep-dog Laddie, a divine animal, always accompanied me. The peace and quiet of this lovely part of Devon, with its ever-changing colours and views of the moors, was entrancing.

My host and hostess were kindness itself to me, with the result that I stayed with them for five years, continuing my professional activities, working at the viola and being kept busy with public performances – in spite of the distance from London. One of my trips to London included an invitation to dinner from Baroness Ravensdale, who was very interested in music. I knew that her guests would consist of distinguished people, especially in the world of art and literature, and that it would be a lovely occasion.

At the dinner table I was seated next to Countess McCormack, wife of the famous Irish tenor, and we were discussing the very latest wireless achievement – Television. In the course of our conversation, I exclaimed with vehemence: 'I think this advent of television is the greatest waster of time so far.' I had noticed that a gentleman sitting two away from me on my left, to whom I had not been introduced, seemed to be very interested in what we were talking about, and when he heard my exclamation he absolutely roared with laughter, leaned over and said to me: 'I don't at all agree with you.' He was none other than Sir Ian Jacob, the then Director-General of the B.B.C.!

Ever since the first Tertis Model had been made in 1938, I had always been on the qui vive to try and seek for betterment in the design in every way possible, most particularly towards facilitating the ease of playing the instrument. I had made quite a few alterations, and by 1953 had come to the conclusion that my final object had been achieved. As a result I gave a recital at the Wigmore Hall with Ruth Fermoy and Bernard Shore, which would display this improved model. Three violas were used. Before the recital, which was in aid of the Musicians' Benevolent Fund, I gave a short address to the audience as follows:

> Since I embarked on this project of a standardized viola in 1937–8 I have concentrated on making this maximum-sized instrument (that is maximum size for playing under the chin) as easy to manage as possible. The length of the viola has not been altered but I have made some six revisions, most of which tend to make it still easier to play upon than the previous model, and any advance in this direction is a great asset to the player. It would take too long to enter into the technical details of the alterations but all these improvements are included in the drawings of which Messrs W. E. Hill & Sons are the sole distributors. I shall be playing on two examples and shall change from one to the other between movements and during movements whenever opportunity occurs, to show that the good tone quality is not confined to just one viola, and also to show the advantage of standard size which permits one to change violas without interfering with one's intonation and without being nonplussed by variations in measurements. I might also mention that the viola on which I shall play the Bach Chaconne is only five weeks old.

The programme consisted of violin sonatas by Padre Martini-Endicott and John Ireland which I had arranged for viola, the Bach Chaconne, my *Variations on a Theme of Handel* for two violas, Brahms's Sonata, Op. 120, No. 2 in E flat, and as encores my piece, *The Blackbirds* and arrangements of *Aria Amorosa* by Galuppi and *Chant de Roxane* by Szymanowski.

The day after the recital I returned to Tavistock and had not been there long before I heard of the Dartington summer school of music (near Totnes, Devon). Never having attended an institution of this kind I thought I would like to find out what it was all about, so off I went and enrolled as a student for a short period. It was there that I met William Glock, who was the director of the summer school, and after about a week or so of my studentship – attending various classes and the splendid nightly concerts – William Glock asked me to undertake the coaching of advanced chamber music players and I eventually became a member of the staff for the annual session of one month, usually in August. I owe a great deal to this event, for there was a sequel to it of magnitudinous import to me, which it will be my pleasure to unfold in due course.

The annual four weeks of summer music-making at Dartington from 1954 to 1957 were a source of most pleasurable satisfaction to me, not only my coaching of chamber music classes of amateur musicians whose love of music was so enthusiastically genuine, but particularly the evening concerts seven times a week, with tip-top programmes by tip-top artists, which somehow or other William Glock miraculously provided. The delightful concert hall was crammed from floor to – I was going to say ceiling, for there were benches arranged in tiers half-way up the walls all around the auditorium. Two of these concerts stand out particularly in my memory, both of them by the famous singer Dietrich Fischer-Dieskau with William Glock at the piano.

I had never heard of Fischer-Dieskau – it must have been among his earliest appearances in this country. He had the most beautiful voice I had ever listened to, with absolutely perfect artistry, and William Glock's exquisite accompanying made them a pair of most evenly matched performers. Incidentally, Fischer-Dieskau is the first and only singer who has moved me to tears. The audiences at these nightly concerts consisted not only of students and staff but people from many miles around the countryside.

In 1954 I lost a great personal friend in the death of Richard Capell, the chief music critic of the *Daily Telegraph*. He was not only a fine and very knowledgeable music critic; he unstintingly and most generously gave his mind to any worthy object that would further the cause of music. I owe him a very deep debt of gratitude not only for his friendship but for his persistent championship of my work which meant so much to me. In 1945 he asked me to write an article which he entitled 'An English Viola' for the magazine *Music and Letters*, of which he was then editor. I was delighted to have this privilege. He also had a great interest in string quartet playing and suggested to me one day that I should contribute a short article on this subject too. I already had many notes concerning it and gladly let him have a few of my ideas on the art of string quartet playing to include in his journal. I have since enlarged that article very considerably and it is included in this book.

It was also in 1954 that, after yet another of my many unsuccessful efforts to discover if there were any good violin craftsmen in Moscow, I conceived the idea of applying to our Foreign Office about the matter. I took courage in both hands and wrote to the Foreign Secretary, Mr Anthony Eden, in response to which he kindly sent me the following answer:

Foreign Office,
S.W.1

July 20, 1954

Sir,

In reply to your letter dated the 6th of July 1954 I am directed by Mr Secretary Eden to advise you that the best method of bringing the specifications and drawings of your new Viola to the attention of the Russian authorities is through Her Majesty's Embassy in Moscow.

If you wish, Mr Eden will be pleased to send the specifications to Her Majesty's Ambassador for transmission through the Soviet Ministry of Foreign Affairs to the Soviet Union of Composers.

I am, Sir,
Your obedient Servant

In reply to this I immediately sent the drawings and specifications to him and again received a letter as follows:

Foreign Office,
S.W.1

July 28, 1954

Sir,

I am directed by Mr Secretary Eden to acknowledge the receipt of your letter dated the 22nd of July 1954, and to inform you that he has now sent the specifications and drawings of your new Viola to Her Majesty's Ambassador at Moscow for transmission through the Soviet Ministry of Foreign Affairs to the Soviet Union of Composers.

I am, Sir,
Your obedient Servant

I acknowledged this letter with deep gratitude. I could have no better introduction to Moscow. But alas! From that day to this I have heard nothing further. Of course it may be that there are *no* craftsmen in Moscow, but the lack of response is still a great disappointment to me. All I can say with regard to the whole matter is that when an important Russian orchestra recently came to give a concert at the Festival Hall I attended the rehearsal, and my attention was immediately drawn to the poor quality of the viola section. In the interval I scrutinized these violas and found most of them to be ridiculously under-sized instruments, quite incapable of producing deep C string sonority.

In 1956 Maurice Eisenberg, the American cellist, was invited by William Glock to give master classes at Dartington, and among the cellists who attended them was a pupil of his, a Miss Lillian Warmington. In my chamber music classes I had two outstandingly competent students – a Norwegian violinist and an excellent English pianist. I particularly wanted to coach a piano trio, a difficult medium to which I have always been rather partial. Eisenberg solved the problem for me by suggesting Miss Warmington as the cellist, whom I found to be very musical and who drew from her cello a lovely expressive tone quality. I thoroughly enjoyed coaching these three professional players, but alas, the team did not last very long, for the violinist became ill and had to return to Norway and my thought of asking Glock if he would consider putting them into one of his evening concerts was thwarted.

Following the four delightful weeks at Dartington, I was invited to spend a month with friends in New York, Professor and Mrs Fairchild. They had a beautiful apartment overlooking the Hudson River. Mary Fairchild was a pupil of mine and a most enthusiastic chamber music player who produced a warm satisfying tone quality from her T.M. viola. She was small in stature, another proof of the ease with which the Tertis Model could be manipulated (yet another being Winifred Copperwheat, a fine viola soloist and excellent teacher who is likewise of small stature and has played on a Tertis Model since 1938). It was a very hectic month including professional engagements, lectures, cocktail parties, sightseeing, etc. – a daily programme from ten in the morning until midnight and after. At the end of the month Mrs Fairchild presented me with a lengthy foolscap paper enumerating the month's activities day by day, and it amused me very much for she had headed it 'Keeping up with Lionel'. That, coming from one of the most energetic Americans I know, I felt was indeed a compliment to a near-octogenarian.

The first professional engagement with which I was involved on this American visit, and in which I made propaganda for the viola as a solo instrument, was a lecture-recital at the Mannes School of Music in New York. Among those present in the audience were a contingent from the Julliard School of Music including Louis Persinger, the great violin pedagogue, Joseph Fuchs, the well-known violinist, our own William Primrose, Rembert Wurlitzer, head of the long-established house of violin-makers of world-wide reputation, and many other professional musicians.

In the course of this sojourn in New York I gave two other lectures and demonstrations, one for the Chamber Music Associates, and the other for the Violin, Viola and Cello Teachers Guild, of which Louis Persinger was the musical director. But the principal object of my trip was to promote my design of viola, and for this purpose I sought an interview with Rembert Wurlitzer with my Tertis Model under my arm. I strode into the office, unpacked my instrument and played on it to show him the qualities. He and his assistant Sacconi, a famous craftsman, were impressed with the tone, and as a result Wurlitzer said he would have a list of violin-makers in America prepared for me. In due course I received this from him with the staggering total of three hundred professional craftsmen, to all of whom I sent a copy of the drawings of the viola, gratis, together with a three-page full detailed specification. The outcome of this free distribution was that up to 1965 there were some sixty makers in the United States alone engaged in making the Tertis Model viola. I have compiled a list of the names and addresses of these craftsmen and other makers in seventeen different countries – which will be found at the end of this book, in case it is of any help to viola-players to know where to get a T.M. viola made or repaired.

My lecture-recital to the Society of Chamber Music Associates was attended by a large gathering of at least three hundred amateur and professional chamber music players at the Brooklyn Academy of Music. My lecture was on string quartet playing and at the end of it I was plied with questions for fully half an hour. I began to think – would I ever be able to answer another one, when suddenly a man stood up at the back of the hall, raised his hand high and said in a stentorian voice: 'Say, Mr Tertis – could you give us the recipe for longevity?' It was such an irrelevant question on so serious a subject as chamber music playing that it completely knocked me off my perch. It took me a moment or two to recover from this alien request. Then I had an inspiration and gave him my recipe in slow measured tones: 'I don't drink – I don't smoke – but I'm not quite a saint!'

A memorable day during this busy month was my unforgettable meeting again with Fritz Kreisler, which took place in the office of his impresario. It was lovely to greet him and we talked of the old days. I had with me a T.M. viola which I was longing to show him. I did not think he had ever seen one, a supposition which proved to be correct. He put it up to his chin and ran his fingers over the fingerboard, remarking on the ease with which he could reach the high positions. Then he said: 'Do you know that at our first rehearsal of the Mozart Sinfonia Concertante here in New York, when you took your instrument out of the case' – (my $17\frac{1}{8}$-inch Montagnana) – 'its enormous size positively frightened me!'

We talked about our performance of the Concertante at the Carnegie Hall and at the opera house in Boston, also the further performance of it at the Albert Hall in London. Altogether this was an imperishable memory for me during that visit to the United States but alas, it was the last time I was to see him. He died in 1962.

On the eve of my departure for home, a pleasant interlude was a visit from Edward Downes, music critic of the *New York Times*. He afterwards wrote an article about our meeting, entitled 'The Quest for the Perfect Viola'. In it he said:

> Hearing Mr Tertis's instrument, one realized why Berlioz chose the solo viola for the hero of his Byronic 'Harold in Italy'. This husky, masculine voice seemed for the moment to have more character than even the rich voice of the 'cello or the infinitely varied and subtle violin.
>
> Looking very un-Byronic in a dark blue business suit, white mustache, glasses and a benign smile, Mr Tertis put his model through additional paces.
>
> The massive multiple stops of the Chaconne from Bach's D minor Partita for unaccompanied violin sound almost more

impressive on the viola. The ghostly sound of this powerful instrument played with a mute is surpassed only by the sound with two mutes, the second being fastened on the bridge beneath the strings . . .

14

Octogenarian Activity

Early in 1957 soon after my eightieth birthday I received tidings of a professional engagement that gave me months of pleasurable anticipation. It was to play at two orchestral concerts on the occasion of the Hallé Centenary Festival the following 30 and 31 October under Sir John Barbirolli. This was only the second time in my life that I had the privilege of playing under J.B.'s baton. The first concert had been in January 1931 with the Scottish Orchestra in Glasgow. I have been probing my mind as to what it was I played, but simply cannot remember the name of the composition. I only know that it was a great joy to play beneath J.B.'s magic wand.

The work I played at the two concerts with the Hallé was the Romance from the Suite for viola and orchestra by Benjamin Dale, with its long continuous tune of no less than thirty-eight bars and middle section containing lively passage work and profuse phrases of subtle rubato – by no means an easy work to conduct. At the second concert I was more in the mood and played better. I indulged, on the inspiration of the moment, in most audacious changes of rubato, phrasing and nuance, and whatever unexpected liberties I took, John was with me, on the dote very time.

In 1957 I received a letter from a friend in America, Paul Doktor – a fine viola-player of New York, to say that he and William Primrose were giving an unusual concert at the Mannes College of Music consisting (with one exception) solely of viola duets, and that he would like to include the Passacaglia on a four-bar theme of Handel which I had written for two violas. William Primrose sent me a copy of the very interesting programme, on the back of which he had written: 'We had a fine concert and many converts to our instrument . . .'

In March 1958 I had a request from a Mr Lewis Harris, a representative in London connected with the Israel Philharmonic Orchestra, asking if I could arrange to send *seven* Tertis Model violas for use in the viola section of the orchestra. I may be forgiven for saying that this wholesale order was very gratifying to me. The letter asked what the cost of the instruments would be and I informed Mr Harris that I had never had any commercial interest in the Tertis Model but that I would write to three craftsmen in the provinces who were making them and ask them to do their utmost to provide the violas as soon as they were able, and that if he would write to them he would get all the information he required. Arthur Richardson of Crediton made two, Saunders of Nottingham made three, and Cocker of Derby made two. In December of that year I received a letter from the viola-players who were using them – Arie Istraeli, Chaim Bor, Yehudith Borochoff, Zeev Steinberg, Daniel Benjamini, Reuven Rottenstein and Marek Rak, principal viola. The letter was signed by Rak.

Dear Maestro,
  We have now received the seven violas and are playing on them with great delight. I consider myself lucky in having secured a Saunders instrument. I might mention that the other day – for the first time in my experience – the conductor said, 'the violas are a little too loud!' This will show you how sonorous is the tone.
  We are very proud and happy that you, dear Maestro, should have taken all the personal care and trouble to ensure that the viola section of the Israel Philharmonic should obtain these fine instruments and on behalf of my colleagues and myself, I wish to express to you our warmest gratitude and thanks . . .

Incidentally I knew that the former leader of the viola section, a Mr Patos, and another player already possessed T.M. violas. Mr Patos eventually came to London and I discovered what a fine player he was, and not only that but he had written two concertos for viola and orchestra, one of which he performed in London. I heard the rehearsal and was delighted to find it a really good work.

A particular memory for me in 1958 was at the annual summer week of the King's Lynn Festival when I took part in Ralph Vaughan Williams's *Flos Campi* ('Flower of the Field' – excerpts from the *Song of Solomon*) for solo viola, small chorus and orchestra. The concert took place in the St Nicholas Chapel, a very large and beautiful early fifteenth-century church, with Herbert Menges, who conducted it very finely indeed. I well remember a rehearsal for this in Vaughan Williams's home in London, with Herbert Menges, followed by another with the chorus (the Linden Singers) and orchestra at Morley College, and I recollect that R.V.W. was not very well at the time but insisted upon coming to it, and that his presence inspired me.

The guiding spirit and creator of the King's Lynn Festival – that unique annual gathering of devotees of music and the arts – is Ruth, Lady Fermoy. King's Lynn was indeed fortunate when the day dawned on which she initiated her first summer week of the Festival in 1951. The ever-growing success of it is the outcome of her never-ceasing enthusiasm, love of culture, indefatigable energy and determination from its inception to the present year as I write.

The high honour is bestowed upon the Festival year by year through the presence of the Queen Mother to whom Ruth Fermoy is Lady-in-Waiting. Her Majesty is Patron of the Festival and attends many of the events that take place during the annual week, and has never missed a Festival since the first one in 1951. The performance of *Flos Campi* on 1 August 1958 was attended by the Queen Mother, who came up to me afterwards when I was in the audience listening to the remainder of the programme and, to my surprise and delight, told me how moved she had been by this beautiful work. It is indeed an extraordinarily fine composition, and the last page particularly contains some of the most lovely music that ever flowed from the pen of R.V.W. Sir Henry Wood gave its first performance at the Queen's Hall in 1925, in which it was my privilege to be the viola soloist. He had numerous rehearsals with the chorus alone, which is a very difficult part of the work.

I had written to Miss Lillian Warmington, whom the reader will remember I had met at Dartington, asking her to come and listen to the performance of *Flos Campi* on 1 August, and she, happily for me, accepted my invitation. Next day, the last of the 1958 Festival, she and I were asked to play in the *Toy Symphony* of Haydn conducted by Gerald Moore. Those who know him can imagine what a frolic he made of it. During the Festival we all stayed at a delightful country hotel some eight miles from King's Lynn, and our party included Lady Fermoy, Gerald Moore and his wife, Herbert Menges and quite a few other artists connected with the Festival.

At the conclusion of the week, Lillian and I left for London from the small country station near the hotel, with our luggage and of course my viola. The reader will, I think, begin to find a clue to the 'sequel' at which I have hinted. We had no sooner taken our seats in the railway carriage and the train was beginning to move slowly out of the station when the guard came along the corridor and presented me with my viola! The porter had spotted it, reclining in its case all alone on the platform seat where Lillian and I had been busily engaged in conversation, run along the platform, and thrust it into the hands of the guard through the luggage van window as the train was moving off. Such was my absorption in Lillian that I could even forget the existence of my beloved and precious viola which had meant so much to me for so many years.

Our destination was Bournemouth, where Lillian resided with her mother, and they had invited me to stay with them for a short holiday. The holiday was far removed from being short – and here let me finally unfold my sequel. A few days later I took courage in both hands and asked Lillian to be my wife. To my unbounded joy, she consented. Our engagement was unofficial, no one knew of it except Lillian's mother, and we arranged for the announcement to appear in the newspapers the day after Lillian, her mother and I were on the high seas bound for South Africa!

Our stay in Cape Town lasted for three months. Among our professional engagements was a recital which Lillian was asked to give for the Cape Town University. Others were a performance of *Flos Campi* when I was fortunate in the conductor – Charles Mackerras, who gave a splendid interpretation of the work; a joint viola and cello recital for the South African Broadcasting Corporation in their concert hall; and a charity concert given by Elsie Hall, the well-known South African pianist, in which we both joined her in chamber music. The rest of the time was spent as a holiday in the lovely warm sunshine and glorious scenery surrounding Cape Town. We were loath to leave it, but a very important event in our lives, for which we had been preparing during our sojourn in South Africa, drew us back to England.

This momentous occasion was our wedding which was to take place at the Musicians' Church, St Sepulchre's in Holborn, on 25 April 1959 – only three weeks after our return from South Africa. The Church of the Holy Sepulchre is the largest parish church in the City and has many associations with music. The Royal School of Church Music was founded there when Sir Sydney Nicholson was organist, and Henry Wood was assistant organist at the age of fourteen. In the north part of the Church lies the Musicians' Chapel containing stained glass windows in memory of Sir Henry Wood, whose ashes are buried in the Chapel, Dame Nellie Melba, and John Ireland, and many other memorials in the shape of chairs and furnishings. Within the Chapel is the Musicians' Book of Remembrance which includes, we are told, over a thousand names.

My dear friend the late Frank Thistleton, secretary of the Musicians' Benevolent Fund – who did so much for this cause and was the moving spirit in the organization for many years – was my best man. We were most fortunate in our fellow-musicians who assisted at the service. The gentlemen of the Choir of St Pauls sang an unaccompanied anthem by Dr Ernest Walker, a setting of the words of Psalm 121: 'I will lift up mine eyes unto the hills' – one of the finest quartet ensembles of voices we had ever heard.

Sir William McKie, the organist of Westminster Abbey, most kindly played the organ for us. During the signing of the register he performed, magnificently, Bach's Prelude and Fugue in B minor. This was followed by three duets for cello and viola which Lillian and I played. The first was the beautiful Psalm 23 'Crimond', the second an 'Elizabethan Melody' of John Dowland, and we ended with an anonymous fifteenth-century folk song with organ accompaniment. It was a unique procedure for bride and bridegroom to play in church at their own wedding, but one which we devoutly felt was an expression of our Thanksgiving to the Almighty.

The reception was held at Lady Fermoy's lovely home in Hyde Park Gardens, and from there we went on a three-week honeymoon to Paris, Rome, Rimini, Venice, Milan, Berne, Lausanne, Geneva and Brussels. As well as meeting friends we were fully occupied calling on violin craftsmen in every city and town we visited, demonstrating the T.M. viola and presenting them all with diagrams and specifications.

Later in September of that year we received an invitation from the President of the Italian Association of Violin-makers, Dr Gioacchino Pasqualini (Professor of Violin and Viola at the Santa Cecilia Academy, Rome), to attend an exhibition devoted entirely to modern violas – the first in musical history – in which over 150 mostly large-sized violas were exhibited from makers in sixteen countries.

On our return from Italy my wife wrote an article describing this visit to the ancient town of Ascoli Piceno, which appeared in *The Strad* in October 1959, entitled 'Italy Honours the Viola'. Here it is slightly abridged.

The town of Ascoli Piceno, chosen for this exhibition, has been in existence for more than two thousand years and has an atmosphere of art and history with Roman and Medieval architecture, a sixteenth-century piazza and treasures from the period 1000 to 1100 AD which few other cities can boast. It lies in a hollow surrounded by hills and mountains one hundred and twenty-four miles from Rome, not far from the Adriatic, and is reached by coach from the capital, a journey of five hours through splendid scenery.

The exhibition was held in the 'Salon' on the first floor of the beautiful seventeenth-century town hall. Half-way up the staircase leading to this room we came face to face with two violas mounted obliquely on the wall bearing between them the word 'Benvenuti'.

On Sunday evening 20 September the official opening took place, and the ceremony was performed by the Minister of Fine Arts, Signor Tupini, who was greeted on his arrival by the town band with a fanfare followed by the National Anthem. In his introductory speech the Minister stressed the importance of the bond of music which binds people of all nations together in friendship and brotherhood and in this case particularly the interest in common of the craftsmanship of violin-making. His remarks proved a very potent message, for a more mixed assembly of nationalities could hardly be imagined than those that followed Signor Tupini into the hall to view this remarkable collection of between one hundred and fifty and one hundred and sixty modern violas.

At this stage of the evening, only a cursory glance at this display of instruments was possible for all were invited to attend a reception given by the town in another ancient building a few minutes walk away. An hour later a concert of music for viols, lutes, etc. was given by the Concentus Fidesque Antiqui group from Rome.

The following morning gave us ample opportunity to examine the fine craftsmanship of many of the instruments, and to discover, much to our gratification, that the vast majority of the violas were of large dimension; indeed, the President of the Associazione Nazionale Liuteria Artistica Italiana – Professor Dr Pasqualini – told us that at a recent referendum he had made, out of 192 professional string players and craftsmen, 181 were in favour of a viola no smaller than 42 centimetres full (16¾ inches).

Two days after the opening, a tour was arranged for all the violin-makers and we found ourselves the only professional string players and incidentally the only English amongst them. We left Ascoli Piceno at 8 a.m. by coach, driving through delightful mountain scenery to the extremely old town of San Ginesio perched high on a hill. A civic reception was held here in the town hall during which Professor Pasqualini presented to the Mayor a violin made by the late Giuseppe Odoardi, a luthier born in the district . . . Following this we were all taken to the church to pay homage to the patron Saint of Cremona violin-makers and stood in silence with the priest at the head of us, by the tomb, which lay under the altar. At the end of this moving experience the Mayor conducted us to a restaurant in the piazza, where with the usual generous Italian hospitality we were regaled with a gargantuan repast. Course after course – innumerable and varied wines prompted some gay and witty speeches in many languages, it was a luncheon of boundless conviviality.

Our stay in Ascoli Piceno ended with a gathering of fiddle-makers, who came to the hotel to see my husband's viola made by Wilfred Saunders of Nottingham. Everyone was impressed with the fine craftsmanship of this instrument and with its sonority and quality of tone. One maker from Mittenwald (Germany), who was an efficient executant, was struck by the ease with which he could move about the instrument. He picked up the viola again and again, giving us quite a large repertoire. Professor Pasqualini also played on it repeatedly and was most enthusiastic. It was as late as 11 p.m. when the gathering insisted on my husband playing, and to my delight he did so with a performance of the Bach Chaconne.

A debt of gratitude is owed to Professor Pasqualini for his untiring efforts and the work that was entailed to bring about this unique exhibition – not to mention the anxiety he went through when some of the instruments were held up by the Customs at the frontier. . . .

Postscript. For me, to my great satisfaction, the Exhibition portends a further eradication of the undersized so-called Viola. Orchestral conductors please note, and eschew small violas. – Lionel Tertis.

In June 1960, under the auspices of the British Council, the then acting Director of Music Miss Avril Wood, daughter of Sir Henry Wood, arranged for my wife and me to give demonstration recitals and broadcasts in Copenhagen, Stockholm and Oslo. These were followed in 1961 by two further similar demonstrations in Madrid and Barcelona. It was at these recitals that my wife first introduced the Tertis Model violoncello, built by Cocker of Derby on similar lines to those of the T.M. viola, but of course in proportion. Miss Avril Wood, like her predecessor Miss Seymour Whinyates, undertook all the arrangements for these recitals, and through her meticulous and painstaking efforts which made everything plain-sailing for us, the result proved to be enthusiastic promotion of the Tertis Models. All the craftsmen we visited in Scandinavia and Spain were given the drawings and specifications of the instruments.

In July 1960 my wife and I had the privilege of playing for the famous girls' school Lawnside at the annual prize-giving which was held in the Winter Gardens, Malvern. This event coincided with the retirement of our friend Miss Winifred Barrows after thirty-five years of wonderful work as headmistress of this school. I also recollect that my friend Leon Goossens, that fine oboist, performed, and Sir Barry Jackson, who shared with Miss Barrows the friendship of Sir Edward Elgar and George Bernard Shaw, gave some very delightful recitations. It was a memorable occasion.

In August we paid a visit to Casals at his summer school which he held in the lovely resort of Zermatt. The Queen of the Belgians, who was staying in Zermatt, was a daily visitor to the Casals classes, being a very keen amateur violinist. My wife joined me in playing unaccompanied duets for viola and cello to the Queen and Casals. Afterwards at the luncheon table, to which Her Majesty did us the honour of inviting us, Casals suddenly turned to me and said: 'You and I must play a duet together on our ninetieth birthday' (we were born on the same day in 1876). Two years later, at a reception given to him by the International Cello Centre in London, where there was a large gathering of cellists and other musicians, I presented him with a proof copy of twenty-six variations for unaccompanied viola and cello which I had written on a four-bar theme of Handel. I warned him that the cello part was *very difficult*. 'But,' I said: 'you *have* got three years to practise it!' Alas! This vista of performing in public with Casals again never materialized, as a year later in 1964, when I was eighty-seven, I definitely gave up playing on the concert platform.

A year after my meeting with Casals in Zermatt, The Musicians' Benevolent Fund generously arranged a luncheon to celebrate my eighty-fifth birthday. Among the messages I received was the following letter from William Walton, the contents of which touched me very much.

San Felice, Forio D'Ischia

27.4.62

My dear Lionel,

I am so very sorry that I am unable to attend the luncheon given in your honour.

All the same I should like to pay tribute to your genius, not only as a superlative virtuoso on the viola, but also for having elevated that somewhat despised and neglected instrument to the high position it now holds, largely through your teaching and guidance, and I doubt if there is a violist present who has not benefited by your inspired example and musical integrity.

Composers also owe you a debt of gratitude in that you encouraged them to write works for the viola, very often written specially for yourself.

So all in all I hope that you can look back over the years of your long career with considerable satisfaction at your great and enduring achievement.

With all good wishes

21 June 1963 was a day of satisfaction to me, for it represented the realization of theories, practice and hopes for the establishment of an *English* string quartet consisting entirely of Tertis Model instruments – the violin and cello made on similar lines (in proportion) to the T.M. viola. To demonstrate the qualities of these instruments,

it was my good fortune to have the services of the Carmirelli String Quartet of Rome who were on a concert tour of this country at the time. I had first met them a good few years previously at a concert at the King's Lynn Festival, when to my astonishment, on going into the artists' room afterwards I had found that they were all playing on Tertis Model instruments made by Cappichioni of Rimini, a very fine craftsman.

For my demonstration concert in 1963 they had only an hour or so at my home to try out the newly-built quartet of instruments (made by Cocker of Derby) before going off to the rehearsal on the morning of the concert. The leader, Miss Pina Carmirelli, brought a Strad which had been loaned to her by the Italian Government, in order to compare it with one of Cocker's violins. She played two excerpts from the Chaconne of Bach, first on the Strad and then on the Cocker T.M. violin, after which she said: 'I think the most important point about these Tertis Model instruments is their timbre which has much more depth than usual. . . . Indeed I think the tone qualities are sensational.' At night she played the complete Chaconne on the T.M. violin, which goes to prove the importance of a standard-sized instrument. In all, three T.M. cellos were used, two violins and two violas. (These instruments were later on exhibition at the 1963 King's Lynn Festival.) The concert was held at the Royal Academy of Music and the proceeds from the purchase of admission programmes were devoted to a prize of a T.M. viola to be competed for by viola students at the R.A.M.

The performance of the new instruments (works by Boccherini and Haydn were played as well as the Bach Chaconne) was commented on with enthusiasm in both general and musical press. *The Times* remarked that 'these modern instruments still sounded amazingly warm and golden'. 'The Tertis Models sounded resonant, smooth and remarkably mature,' commented *The Strad*, and *Musical Opinion*: 'The results were wholly satisfactory, and it was proved without a shadow of doubt that the Violin, with its richly mellow tone, is fully the equal of its predecessors.' Martin Cooper, whose review in the *Daily Telegraph* was headlined 'Tertis Model Triumph', wrote:

Both violins and cellos made an extremely favourable impression, for at something like one-tenth of the price they reproduce much of the depth, roundness and fullness of tone hitherto considered unobtainable except on instruments made by the great 18th-century masters.

The cellos were particularly striking and Lillian Tertis's performance of her husband's arrangement of an Adagio from Bach's Easter Oratorio, accompanied by Sir Thomas Armstrong, demonstrated the new instrument's sensitiveness to every smallest inflection of phrase and gradation of *piano* tone.

At the 1963 King's Lynn Festival we once again had the wonderful opportunity of hearing Sir John Barbirolli conduct his two annual concerts. We heard him in the St Nicholas Chapel. His music-making was invariably lovely, exciting, thrilling. One of the most memorable of his interpretations was his conducting of the *Symphonie Fantastique* of Berlioz with the Hallé Orchestra – the finest performance of this work I have ever heard. I am reminded of another concert that lives in my memory, one at the 1957 King's Lynn Festival when Evelyn Rothwell (Lady Barbirolli) played magnificently the oboe concerto in C by Haydn, accompanied by the London Mozart Players with Sir John conducting. Evelyn Rothwell is a superlative artist. Her immaculate technique and pure expressive tone quality are great joys to experience. At yet another Festival I shall ever remember Sir John's performance of his beautiful transcription for orchestra of Bach's Chorale Prelude 'In our hour of deepest need'. This great and sincere artist subsequently fulfilled a promise then made to send me a copy of the published score and honoured me beyond words by writing upon it the following inscription of which I am very proud: 'To my very dear friend Lionel Tertis, who "in our hour of deepest need" restored the viola to us. – John.'

The 1963 Festival is also imprinted on my mind for my wife's performance at the Festival Service in St Margaret's Church. She chose the beautiful Adagio from Bach's *Easter Oratorio* which I had arranged for cello and organ. She played in the transept out of sight of the congregation, and the effect of this glorious melody of Bach in the beautiful building with its marvellous acoustic properties was quite ethereal and most moving.

It has been my privilege to make music with Lady Fermoy at a number of her Festivals, and to attend others as a member of the audience; indeed I think I missed only two festivals through indisposition from 1952 to 1970. One of these was in 1965, when we

Playing at a Hallé Centenary season concert, 1957— twenty years younger than the Orchestra (left); laying down the law to R.V.W. about a forthcoming performance of Flos Campi, 1958 (right)

The International Exhibition of Modern Violas at Ascoli Piceno, September 1959. Nearest the camera are Signor Tupini, Italian Minister of Fine Arts (with outstretched arm) and Dr Gioacchino Pasqualini, President of the Italian Association of Violin-Makers (right)

Photograph given to the author by Queen Elisabeth of the Belgians. Inscribed: 'To the great and dear Artist Lionel Tertis in remembrance of La Panne 1915 with Ysaÿe and Zermatt Sept. 1961'

At Pablo Casals's Summer School in Zermatt, 1961. The author and Casals congratulate each other on their joint birthday (both were born on 29 December 1876)

With Sir John Barbirolli,
King's Lynn, 1968. The
folder of this photograph is
inscribed: 'For dearest Lillian
—This picture which I
treasure, for I think it does
show two fairly aged musicians
who I suspect adore each
other'

Patron and Chairman of the
King's Lynn Festival arrive
at the Guildhall, 30 July
1969: Queen Elizabeth the
Queen Mother and Ruth,
Lady Fermoy

The author, aged ninety, gives a speech at E.M.I. House on the release of a record selecting some of his recordings of the 'Twenties and 'Thirties

The author at his home with Arthur Rubinstein, 1973, discussing the proofs of the latter's autobiography (left the author in his ninety-eighth year (right)

journeyed to King's Lynn but instead of enjoying a week of concerts I was confined to my room in the hotel with influenza. I had looked forward to a particular programme in which Rostropovich was performing with orchestra in the St Nicholas Chapel. Instead, my wife went to the morning rehearsal and gave him from me a copy of the lovely melody I had arranged from the *Easter Oratorio* for cello and organ.

After the evening concert he insisted upon coming to the hotel to greet me – taking no notice of his wife's protests (for they were motoring to London that same night where he had a rehearsal at the Festival Hall next morning). Casting discretion to the winds he burst into my room, where he found me enveloped in a dressing-gown and with a temperature – in spite of which he embraced me! I had never met him in my life but I can only presume he must have known of me through broadcasts or records. What a great artist and a wonderful character he is. One has only to think of the way he defended Solzhenitsyn in his own country – and I shall never forget his splendid speech (in quite good English) when the Royal Philharmonic Society, at one of their concerts, presented him with their Gold Medal.

I had reached the age of eighty-seven when the London Philharmonic Orchestral Society's Club invited me to give a short lecture-demonstration of the T.M. instruments. This took place in the Arts Council's lovely room in St James's Square. My wife and I played unaccompanied duets for cello and viola. (Incidentally my wife discarded her fine Testore cello in preference for a Tertis Model which she has used since it was first made in 1962. It was entirely her own choice without any persuasion whatever from me!) At this demonstration we were assisted by Antonio Brosa and Leonard Hirsch using two T.M. violins on which they played the Bach D minor double concerto. In my lecture I pointed out a few of the unorthodox features that I had conceived for the T.M. viola. This London Philharmonic Society meeting was my last public appearance with my viola on the concert platform. Unlike the Prima Donna I have indulged in only two farewell concerts – one in 1937 due to rheumatism, and this other in 1964 due to Anno Domini.

A month later the Royal Philharmonic Society conferred upon me the great honour of the Society's Gold Medal which thrilled me beyond words, and a further jubilation – that it was presented in person by Sir John Barbirolli at the Society's last concert of their season on 22 April 1964. After I had received the medal from Sir John, I spoke to the audience in the following terms:

I must confess it is somewhat unnerving to find myself in rather an extraordinary situation tonight. Here am I on the platform at the Royal Philharmonic Society concert, being awarded the highest musical distinction, and getting away with it without scraping a tune! [For this medal is generally given to an artist who, at the time it is awarded, has performed at a concert.] Be that as it may, I do so want to express my gratitude to the Royal Philharmonic Society for the honour they have done me, and I am sure my fellow viola-players will allow me to speak on their behalf as well as my own in saying how much we exult in the fact that the Society's Gold Medal has given a further tremendous uplift to the importance and status of our beloved instrument, and as a consequence it now has a real place in the sun.

15

Revolutionary Seating Plan for a Symphony Orchestra

For many years, as long ago as the 1920s, I had had a plan in mind for drastic changes in the seating layout of a symphony orchestra in order to obtain better balance of tone between strings, brass, percussion and woodwind. This was the result of my very early efforts of recording for the gramophone. I had two reasons for hoping for a better balance of orchestral tone.

(1) In the early days of recording I had to play into a sort of elongated post horn, and I found that if I played into it at right angles (the usual position), the quantity of tone produced on a gramophone record was not as great as when I faced the horn – i.e. with the scroll of the viola pointing at the horn.

(2) I had noticed when listening in the auditorium that when a violin soloist plays to the conductor, at right angles to the audience, the tone from his violin is of smaller quantity than when he at times faces the auditorium, i.e. with scroll pointing to the audience. I submit also that in the orthodox seating of the strings of the orchestra, the f holes (or sound holes) of the instruments in most cases face in opposite directions – one f hole emitting sound into the auditorium, and the sound from the other f hole being considerably wasted, towards the back of the platform.

All this influenced me in my idea to seat the string players so that *as many of them as possible* faced the auditorium with their instruments, as depicted on the diagram on the next page. Most orchestral concert halls differ in shape and layout, therefore amendments may have to be made, for example, in the height of the conductor's rostrum so that he can see all the players to his satisfaction, and all players can see the conductor. But the priority should always be that the scrolls of the string instruments should point to the auditorium as much as possible.

123

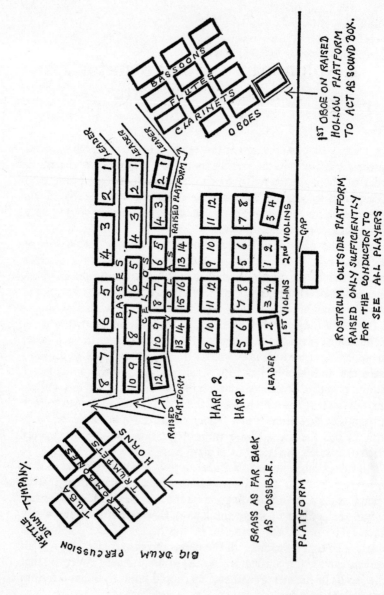

Revolutionary seating plan for a symphony orchestra

When I broached the subject to my dear friend Sir John Barbirolli, he was as ever ready to probe into anything that might mean progress and generously arranged, together with the Hallé Society, to give the plan a trial, and this took place in the Free Trade Hall, Manchester on 2 May 1964. The result of the trial was that the consensus of opinion did not *entirely* agree with my contention that better balance would result – but I still stick to it that it would. The difficulty of balance of tone in the normal position of the orchestra is particularly evident in passages when the brass and wind are playing with full force, obliterating a large measure of string tone which is important and thus ruining the balance.

John asked me to say a few words to the audience before the trial, which I did. But I took the precaution of informing them that if I thought the experiment a failure, I would effect my escape by a prepared route through one of the back doors. My idea, which evidently I did not make plain to dear Sir John, was to have *short excerpts*, from works where the strings were submerged to a considerable extent, played in the two different positions, changing over with as little noise and as quickly as possible so that the different effects of orthodox and unorthodox seating could be accurately grasped. Instead of which, first of all to my astonishment I found the occasion had been made an invitation concert and the hall was full of people; and then, as far as my memory serves me, two *whole works* – Strauss's *Don Juan* and Berlioz's *Carnaval Romain* – were played with my seating, and *after an interval* the works were repeated in the orthodox seating, which of course made it impossible to form an adequate judgement owing to the long interval between orthodox and unorthodox seating.

The critic of the *Manchester Guardian* wrote: 'The new position certainly encouraged a vivid and brilliant upper string tone, though rather at the expense of the lower strings', and the critic of the *Manchester Evening News* in similar terms: 'I liked the new sound for its dazzling violin tone, but I found it hard to pick out the lower strings.' The cause of this imbalance was quite simply that there was *by no means* a full complement of cellos or double basses on that day. Michael Kennedy wrote in the *Daily Telegraph* that 'with modifications Mr Tertis's ideas certainly seem to be worth serious consideration.'

However, I shall always be grateful to Sir John and the Hallé for their willingness to undertake this experiment towards improvement of the balance of tone in the orchestra, which was an expensive operation. I hope that one day some affluent reader who by chance might be perusing this, or some beneficent organization that might hear of the idea, will feel interested to have another dig at it – always bearing in mind the principal important factor, the strings facing the auditorium as much as possible. And I reiterate that only *short* excerpts should be performed, first in the orthodox position and second in my unorthodox position. When the conductor has tried this out to his satisfaction, his deputy should conduct the same excerpts in the same order and the conductor proper should listen to it from the auditorium.

I find an entry in my diary for 24 June 1964 – an invitation from Sir Ashley Clarke, former British Ambassador in Rome, and Lady Clarke to a delightful supper party at their home. My friend William Glock was among the guests and in the course of conversation he told me of what I considered a most brilliant idea of his, that of instituting a B.B.C. training orchestra – which actually came into being soon after.

It has long been in my mind that we have on the professorial staffs of our musical academies and colleges string players of experience and distinction who are not only capable of teaching technique and concerto-playing, etc. to embryo instrumentalists, but who know the monumental orchestral library from A to Z, and all the tricks of the trade. In several auditions which I have undertaken, I have heard scores of capable instrumentalists, but with few exceptions they were a dismal failure when called upon to tackle almost anything in the orchestral library, of which they had a very sparse knowledge. The music for orchestra bristles with most difficult passage work which alone will develop technical capability. What I am getting at is that part of the teacher's lesson time should be devoted to the study of orchestral parts in which the budding instrumentalist is concerned, and which he can practise. By this means a body of players would be built up already trained to some extent in orchestral music, which would facilitate their upbringing in this splendid institution of a training orchestra. I wonder whether this is done nowadays, or done enough? If not, why not?

Among the many competitions I have adjudicated, none gave me greater pleasure than the first violin competition organized by the

B.B.C. in April 1965. My fellow-adjudicators were Alfredo Campoli and Sydney Griller. Afterwards I wrote a letter to the *Daily Telegraph* praising the talent of young British violinists that the competition had revealed, and ended by saying: 'It would be a splendid move towards encouraging British embryo virtuosi if further competitions on the same lines could be instituted by the B.B.C. for the various other solo instrumentalists.'

It was to be my gratification to find that in the 1970 International Carl Flesch Violin Competition, which was part of the City of London Festival, viola-players were included for the first time (I believe at the instigation of my friends Yehudi Menuhin and Yfrah Neaman), so making musical history as far as England is concerned. I attended the finals of the competition as a listener, and it was an added pleasure for me that the second and third prizes were captured by viola soloists. To my further satisfaction and pleasure, violas were again included in the 1972 competition, and what is more – two viola soloists ousted all the violin competitors to bag first and second prizes. When I heard this news I felt like imitating the joyful sound of the early morning cock crow!

I should also like to see instituted an International Composers' Competition for works for viola solo and orchestra.

16

Nonagenarian Activity

On 29 December 1966 I reached my ninetieth birthday and both the B.B.C. and the Royal Philharmonic Society did me the great honour of celebrating the occasion.

The B.B.C. in the afternoon broadcast the following programme and I introduced the items:

Sinfonia Concertante in E flat (K.364)   Mozart

Albert Sammons   (violin)
Lionel Tertis   (viola)
London Philharmonic Orchestra conducted by Sir Hamilton Harty*

Gramophone record

Variations on a Four-bar Theme of Handel
for viola and cello   Tertis

Harry Danks   (viola)
Lillian Tertis   (cello)

Trio Op. 87 for three violas   Beethoven
                                                         arr. Tertis

Cecil Aronowitz   (viola)
Harry Danks   (viola)
Margaret Major   (viola)

---

* E.M.I. made, also in celebration of my ninetieth birthday, a record (Great Instrumentalists No. 2) with this performance on one side and various short viola solos of mine on the other. The short pieces were taken from old 78 Columbia records from which E.M.I. had practically eradicated the scratch accepted in the early days by recording companies and public alike.

Praeludium and Allegro   Kreisler (after
                                                         Pugnani) arr.
                                                         Tertis

         Lionel Tertis   (viola)
         Ethel Hobday   (piano)
Gramophone record

At night I was guest of honour at the Royal Philharmonic Society's
dinner at the Connaught Rooms, and the celebration coupled my
name with that of my 'twin' Casals. We have more than once been
alluded to as the 'Heavenly Twins', but I cannot lay claim to such
an exalted status, for the great Maestro was far more heavenly than
I am.

Sir Thomas Armstrong was in the chair and the other speakers
were Sir Edward Boyle, M.P., and my life-long friend Sir John
Barbirolli. It would be embarrassing for me to quote what they said,
but I will mention that Sir Thomas read out a few preliminary lines
from a poem he had written for the occasion, in which he praised
my humble efforts far in excess of my capabilities. I was overcome
with embarrassment at having to follow these three illustrious
speakers – but here is the gist of what I replied.

'My very good friends,' I began, for the customary 'Ladies and
Gentlemen' was too cold and formal for me to express my deep feeling of gratitude. I mentioned my debt to the R.P.S. for having had
me play at a considerable number of their concerts over the years,
which had been such an immense help to me in my campaign for
the viola as a solo instrument. I passed on my recipe for longevity:
'*Take up the viola!*' I reminded Sir Thomas Armstrong that I had
attended the school of which he was now Principal, the R.A.M., and
that it was there that I had been introduced to the viola. Turning to
Sir Edward Boyle, who I had heard was a keen amateur musician,
I said I envied him, for to be an amateur had long been an ambition
of mine, for the reason that you could play what you liked, when
you liked, how you liked, or not at all if you didn't like. Finally I
said how touched I was that Sir John Barbirolli should have come
to the dinner on the eve of his epoch-making visit to the Soviet
Union with the B.B.C. Symphony Orchestra to preach the gospel of
his wonderful art.

Among the telegrams I had the great honour to receive one from

10

the Queen Mother: 'Warmest congratulations on your 90th birthday I hope you will have a very happy day.' Others came from Pablo
Casals, Edward Heath, Sir Malcolm Sargent, the Mayor and
Citizens of my birthplace, West Hartlepool – and this from Arthur
Rubinstein in New York: 'Dearest Lionel accept my heartfelt
wishes for your glorious anniversary, and please read out my Toast
at the Royal Philharmonic Dinner "To one of the greatest musicians
of my life-time and my dearest friend". Love – Arthur Rubinstein.'

In September 1967 my wife and I journeyed once more to South
Africa for a further visit to Cape Town, laden with five T.M. instruments (two violins, two cellos and a viola) plus the drawings of them.
On board ship on the first evening of the trip, the Captain following
the usual custom invited the passengers to a cocktail party. His greet-
ing to me on my being introduced to him was: 'Oh! You are the
famous fiddler – in more ways than one I expect!'

The particular object of our journey was to make South Africa
the sixteenth country in which the T.M. viola would, I hoped, be
made. But to my amazement there was no expert violin craftsman
in Cape Town with whom I could discuss the project, so vitally
necessary to their symphony orchestra and the colleges of music
there – to say nothing of the amateur string players. If anything
went wrong with their instruments the players had to send them to
Johannesburg (1,000 miles), Durban (1,000 miles) or to London
(6,000 miles!) with all the dangers of transit to these distant parts
and consequent unconscionable delay for repair. I suggested in a
letter to the *Cape Times* that a talented young South African wood-
worker should be sent for instruction to the famous school of violin-
making in Mittenwald, Germany. He would return after the three
years' course of study a good violin craftsman able to attend to all
the wants of the string players in Cape Town. Whether any result
came of this letter I do not know.

This visit to Cape Town was a busman's holiday for both my wife
and myself, for the Cape Town Symphony Orchestra were very
short of cellists (instead of at least eight, there were only four), so
my wife gallantly stepped into the breach, playing as a member of
the orchestra at all the symphony concerts during our stay of over
three months. She thoroughly enjoyed her new role of orchestral
playing, and becoming conversant with a tremendous slice of the

cellist's orchestral library, while I enjoyed myself attending almost daily rehearsals as a listener and meeting the conductor, Derek Hudson.

Later in the following year, after our return from South Africa, my wife and I visited our friends in Malvern, Miss Winifred Barrows and Miss Jane Parke. During our stay they made the suggestion that we should drive over to Elgar's birthplace some few miles distant – for which we shall ever be grateful. We were simply enthralled by what we saw: a most charming cottage in which all Elgar's precious belongings had been wonderfully assembled and displayed with loving care by the then curator Alan Webb and his wife. The small room on the ground floor had been arranged to represent in some degree the study in one of his homes where he created his glorious compositions. My emotions were deeply stirred to see his desk, and the actual chair on which he sat, in the same position as when I had visited him in Stratford-on-Avon in 1932 to play to him my arrangement for viola of his cello concerto.

As a result of my thrilling experience I wrote a letter of appeal to the *Daily Telegraph* pleading for contributions towards the fund for the upkeep of the Elgar Birthplace. The *Daily Telegraph* was on this occasion as generous as it has been on the innumerable others when it has afforded me – and the viola – space in its columns. My letter was given a prominent place in the Saturday edition (2 November 1968), the day of the week when musical events are conspicuously displayed.

Sir – One of the great treasures of Britain is the birthplace of Sir Edward Elgar at Broadheath, near Worcester.

Recently, on a visit to this modest home, I was truly moved and overjoyed to find it filled with all the manuscripts, letters, decorations and all manner of precious belongings spanning the life of this great composer – *all* of untold value to the nation.

This home should be preserved as one of our most important national monuments. As long ago as 1934 the *Daily Telegraph* initiated an appeal under the chairmanship of the late Sir Landon Ronald to found the Elgar Birthplace Trust, which resulted in raising some £2,500.

Just over a year ago the appeal was 'revived' by my colleague Yehudi Menuhin. For this donations and subscriptions are still being sought so that ultimately a sum of £25,000 may be achieved which would serve to maintain Sir Edward's home for all time. I therefore humbly venture to make the following suggestions toward the realisation of this goal:

1. All students of our academies and colleges of music both here and in the Commonwealth, all my orchestral colleagues in the symphony orchestras of the world and indeed all music-lovers would, I am sure, be interested and find it possible to express their interest in donating the small sum of 5s, and those who felt so moved, and could afford it, multiples of that amount.

2. If their respective rules permit, might not the Arts Council, the Royal Society of Musicians, the British Council, the Performing Right Society, the B.B.C. and other institutions contribute toward this incalculably important project?

3. A reminder – by the Tourist Information Centre (and their offices overseas) to our American, Commonwealth and other overseas friends who all but invariably visit Shakespeare's birthplace at Stratford-on-Avon – that Broadheath is but a very short distance away. Could this not be stated in their literature?

A suggestion which has, by coincidence, reached me simultaneously from two friends of mine – Sir Arthur Bliss, our Master of the Queen's Musick, and Miss Winifred Barrows, retired headmistress of 'Lawnside' in Malvern – is their wonderful idea of the publication of a postage stamp depicting Sir Edward and issued on the birthday of the composer, June 2, next year.

May I as a nonagenarian selfishly implore the Postmaster-General to perform some miracle of rearrangement which would enable him to give this issue priority, in the hope that I may have the chance of seeing it in circulation next June?

Illustrated brochures can be obtained free of charge from the Elgar Birthplace Trust Appeal Office, 91a Grosvenor Road, S.W.1., Tel: 01-834 2858.

Yours faithfully

Entirely from this letter of appeal, over one thousand pounds was immediately forthcoming, which included among many donations the munificent sum of five hundred pounds from the Performing Right Society. But no Elgar postage stamp was issued, no such event as a centenary being involved.

Soon after my memorable visit to Elgar's birthplace, I listened to a most beautiful performance of his violin concerto. The soloist was Alfredo Campoli with the B.B.C. Scottish Orchestra conducted by James Loughran. Among the numerous times I have heard this wonderful work, so full of lyrical moments that stir one to the depths, this performance of Campoli's was certainly the best I have ever heard.

In June 1969, out of the blue, Sir John Barbirolli telephoned me to say he was going to conduct at the Casals Festival in Puerto Rico. With his usual kindliness he told me the idea had come to him that it would be rather nice if I would write a message to my fellow-nonagenarian, and he would undertake to deliver it. Needless to say I jumped at this suggestion and was overcome, to say the least of it, with the thought of having such an illustrious postman.

In reply the following letter came from Pablo Casals which was a great joy to receive and meant much to me.

> Isla Verde K2 – H3
> Santurce, Puerto Rico
> June 23, 1969

My dear friend,
How happy I was to receive your dear letter! Many times I think of you and of the times we made music together. It was always a joy and a privilege for me to play with you. I wish so much that we may meet again!

Our dear mutual friend Sir John was magnificent at our Festival. It was a great experience for me to hear his Mahler Symphony and I was deeply moved. I had never heard such a performance of this work. And, of course, needless to say, we were both so happy and moved to be with one another again.

I hope that you are keeping well and that you continue to make music, I have wonderful reports about your health and I pray God that you may continue to enjoy it for many years with your good wife.

Marta and I send our heartiest wishes to you both.

> With my affection and admiration,
> [signed] Pablo Casals

To Maitre Lionel Tertis
London, England

After becoming a nonagenarian I did not of necessity go out to evening concerts, but I always made one exception to the rule – I would not, as long as I had one leg to stand upon, miss a recital in London where Arthur Rubinstein was concerned, because it was always the most thrilling musical experience for me. The last recital of his I attended was on 15 June 1970, when at the age of eighty-two he played, if anything, more wonderfully than ever. When I saw him after the concert in the artists' room, he told me a little about the colossal schedule of engagements and travelling following this recital, which made me gasp. I asked him where he got the strength to do it all, and to play such an ever-changing and immense repertoire. His immediate reply was, 'Well, it's better than twiddling my thumbs!' How right he is.

Just over a month after Arthur Rubinstein's recital a calamity befell the musical world in the sudden death of Sir John Barbirolli. It was a shattering blow; at the age of seventy, he had been in the prime of life. Apart from his technical mastery and his brilliant gift of interpretation, the most significant thing for me was his extraordinary power to draw forth the lovely warmth of expression and tone quality from whatever orchestra he conducted. The magic of his baton has ever been a source of inspiration to me, and his memory will never fade. He has been one of the greatest ambassadors for music that England has ever possessed.

A lovable feature of his character was his constant readiness to help young musicians. In spite of his hectic life he undertook to conduct the weekly practices of the student orchestra at his old school the Royal Academy of Music, and taught them all the tricks of the trade with the utmost kindness and tolerance. He also found time to head a panel of adjudicators, of which I was a member, to judge the merits of very young cellists who were applying for grants from the Suggia gift. (Guilhermina Suggia, the famous cellist who died in 1950, left in her will a considerable sum of money for the purpose of helping young, very talented cellists to obtain the best pedagogical assistance, in the hope of producing star exponents of her instrument.) These adjudications, so admirably administered by the Arts Council, were held in the afternoon in the empty Wigmore Hall, and Sir John invariably went up to the platform to give each applicant a kindly word of encouragement both before and after they played.

To follow with another sadness for me – in the waning of that same year, 1970, I was compelled, owing to indisposition, to forgo for the first time in very many years a recital in London by Arthur Rubinstein. However, he filled me with unbounded joy by telephoning from Paris some two or three weeks after his recital saying that he would come and see me at my home at 3 pm on 7 December. His visit coincided with a strike of the electrical engineers. We were unaware that the front door bell did not ring owing to the black-out. He had been 'practising his finger exercises on the bell' for an unconscionable time, so he later told us, when a neighbour saw his difficulties and telephoned us. We had been waiting for him for quite half an hour, and our joy may be imagined at seeing him when we rushed to open the front door. The only illumination in our home was by dim candlelight.

In the course of our conversation I bemoaned my fate at having missed his London recital. A day or two after this lovely visit, to my astonishment there arrived two huge parcels. One contained records of his playing of concertos, sonatas, mazurkas, etc., and of his performances in piano quartets and quintets with the Guarneri String Quartet. The second parcel housed a stereo record-player. Needless to say I was overcome with this wonderful gift, which enabled me to command a recital of his whenever I wished.

The following year I worked at intervals at my autobiography until my ninety-fifth birthday on 29 December. And two days later the New Year of 1972 came in most auspiciously with the high honour of an invitation from Mr Heath to a dinner he was giving at 10 Downing Street in celebration of Sir William Walton's seventieth birthday on 29 March.

At the reception in the ante-room before the dinner I was feeling very apologetic to be the only person sitting down, when suddenly the Prime Minister came up to me with the Queen Mother. I had had no idea that she was going to be present. Somehow I got to my feet alone and so overjoyed was I that I involuntarily took her hand in both my hands, I should say for quite a minute, and during this time she never attempted to take her hand away.

After the reception we went into the dining-room. An extraordinary episode occurred at dinner. The repast began with a delectable cup of soup, following which a hot plate was placed in front of me with what looked like a scrumptious morsel. My wife, whom as usual I had specially asked to be seated next to as I needed her to dissect my food because of my very faulty vision, was engaged in conversation with her neighbour, and I thought I would attack this dish on my own initiative. I began poking at it with my fork but could not pick it up. She suddenly turned and saw what I was trying to do and whispered to me: 'For Heaven's sake put your fork down! There's nothing on your plate . . . you are digging at the coat of arms!' Fortunately my antics had not been noticed, the tables being lit by subdued candlelight.

For much of 1972 I had had in mind a viola concert of unusual character and I brought this to fruition on my birthday on 29 December at the Wigmore Hall. The programme consisted of a suite for one viola by Max Reger, a duet for violas (my own *Variations on a Four-bar Theme of Handel*), a trio for violas by Beethoven, a quartet for violas by York Bowen, a Concertante for five violas by Kenneth Harding, and an Introduction and Andante for six violas by B. J. Dale. These were all unaccompanied and the players were the viola section of the B.B.C. Symphony Orchestra.

Harry Danks, who first became a pupil of mine in 1935, performed the Herculean task of leading in all six compositions, some of which were difficult technically, and organizing the other eleven players for the scanty rehearsals they were able to have, for the reason that my concert took place not only in Christmas week and on a Friday afternoon, but it was the week of the B.B.C.'s Winter Promenade concerts. I owe a debt of gratitude to them all for so generously helping at my birthday concert in such a strenuous week.

It was a particular pleasure to me to have Messrs Ibbs & Tillett manage the concert, for they have been my sole agents throughout the whole course of my career since 1922. It was an intricate concert and all the complicated preparations were splendidly organized by Ibbs & Tillett; their kindness helped to swell the proceeds which were donated to the Samaritan Fund of the Royal Society of Musicians. The hall was full, even on a Friday afternoon.

Fortunately the day was extraordinarily mild and, antediluvian creature that I am, I was thankfully able to be present (although I had intended to get there even to the extent of employing an ambulance). At the end of the programme I ventured to say a few words to the audience. 'My piece in this programme is for solo voice,' I began, 'and it is marked *Molto Adagio con espressione*, but, let me hasten to allay your apprehension, it is only two or three bars long.' I went on to thank the players and to refer to the wonderful traditions of the Royal Society of Musicians. (For example, on 23 March 1743 Handel performed *Messiah* for this beneficent Society and conducted the first English performance at Covent Garden, the funds from which were given to the R.S.M. In his will Handel left £1,000 for the Society which also benefited from performances of *Messiah* every year, and from the great Handel Commemoration Festivals given annually in Westminster Abbey.)

When I had finished my speech, to my surprise the viola-players began the tune 'Happy Birthday to you!' and the audience sang this original and *brainy* composition with such fervour that I felt obliged to comment on their performance and blurted out: 'Throughout the whole course of my long life I have never heard this *difficult, intricate* choral work more splendidly rendered!'

The concert was noticed in *The Times*. Here is the end of William Mann's review:

> Tertis persuaded York Bowen to write a Fantasie for a string quartet of violas, which was played in this concert. The bass line cannot descend farther than C below middle C, but the limitation is barely perceived, so rich and multifarious are the textures available. This is a finely imagined movement in several sections, often twilit and nostalgic (with a touch of modality, that doffs the cap to Debussy's quartet), worth hearing several times. So is Benjamin Dale's Introduction and Andante for six violas, composed in 1911 and naturally reminiscent of a period that we know best in Schoenberg's *Verklärte Nacht*, ripe late romanticism, most attractive.
>
> A Concertante for five violas by Kenneth Harding made gallant, exhilarating noises and sounded fun to play though probably difficult. Tertis himself was represented as composer by his variations on a theme by Handel, very virtuoso and full of individual opportunities for two viola players; and by his transcription of Beethoven's opus 87 trio from woodwind to violas; it sounds more enjoyable in this viola version, strange as this may seem.
>
> Violas, we were reminded, are versatile as well as tonally alluring and capable of virtuosity. The performances sounded under-rehearsed, sometimes almost casual, but full of spirit.

My reader will now have gathered some idea of my journey through life, and my pen waits impatiently to pay tribute with deep gratitude to the all-powerful media which have consistently supported the fight for the once-upon-a-time 'Cinderella'. First, the *Daily Telegraph*, who have never failed to champion the cause from the end of the nineteenth century to the present day, which has helped enormously to raise the status of the viola as a solo instrument. Secondly, the B.B.C., who since their formation have made it possible for countless *laymen* as well as the musical profession to hear the characteristic qualities of the viola as a solo instrument, thus further establishing it in its rightful place for all time.

A further satisfaction to me is that there are well over six hundred T.M. violas in circulation, and that they are now being made in seventeen different countries.

It is also with gratification that I pay tribute to the many viola players who have taken up the torch I ventured to light in 1895, and have carried on the campaign to establish the viola as a solo instrument. To mention only a few in alphabetical order, I call to mind:

The South African Cecil Aronowitz, a splendid teacher and fine musician, principally a chamber music player, who has taken up the important position of Head of String Studies at the Royal Northern College of Music, Manchester. Harry Berly, one of the best pupils I ever had who died prematurely. Winifred Copperwheat, a pupil of mine who is still teaching at the Royal Academy of Music and by the way, plays on a T.M. 16¾-inch viola with *ease* in spite of her small stature. Paul Cropper, another pupil, who has led the violas in the B.B.C. Northern Symphony Orchestra since 1945. Harry Danks, again a pupil of mine, who since 1946 has been leader of the viola section of the B.B.C. Symphony Orchestra; he is also a protagonist of the viola d'amore, for many years led an ensemble called the London Consort of Viols, which gave one hundred and fifty broadcasts, and is now busily engaged in writing a history of the viola d'amore. Herbert Downes, that splendid solo violist who has been leader of the Philharmonic Orchestra from 1945 until 1973. Sidney Errington, again my pupil who recently retired after very many years as principal violist in the Hallé Orchestra; he extolled the virtues of the viola as a solo instrument whenever the opportunity came his way, and he is now a member of the music panel of the Yorkshire Arts Association, an offshoot of the Arts Council, and is still doing splendid teaching work.

We all know that champion of the viola William Primrose, about whom I have already spoken; Frederick Riddle, another splendid soloist who used to lead the violas in the London Philharmonic Orchestra and now those of the Royal Philharmonic Orchestra; and Peter Schidlof, the fine violist of the Amadeus String Quartet of which Norbert Brainin is the leader – often have I enjoyed the magnificent performances of these two musicians in Mozart's Sinfonia Concertante. My pupil Bernard Shore, who from 1930 to 1943 was leader of the B.B.C. Symphony Orchestra, subsequently becoming music inspector at the Ministry of Education, has ever preached the gospel of the viola as a solo instrument in his innumerable lectures.

In the United States, Tom Brennand, another pupil and principal viola of the Cleveland Orchestra, Paul Doktor, a magnificent player of chamber music, soloist and teacher, and the distinguished soloist Lillian Fuchs (sister of Joseph Fuchs) keep the flag flying for the solo viola. Then there are Milton Katims and Samuel Lifshey, one-time principal violists of the Philadelphia Orchestra, William Linier, Spinoza Paeff (Baltimore), Joseph de Pasquale (Boston), Milton Preves (Chicago) and Walter Trampler. In Israel, there is Odeen Patos (Tel Aviv). Many others have been 'bagged' as principals in the innumerable fine orchestras that now exist the world over, with the result that they have little time to spare in which to indulge in concerto playing.

Owing to the insatiable demand for violas at the present time W. E. Hill & Sons have very recently begun to make them, which is a source of great satisfaction for my cause. The beautiful string instrument cases they have made since about 1820 are positive works of art, and known throughout the world. Desmond Hill, the present head of W. E. Hill, is not only a master craftsman but an inventor as well. A recent example is the lightest and most substantial cello case I know of, suitable for modern-day travel, and he has also produced a viola case which can be adjusted to fit any-sized viola between 16 inches and 17 inches. Both he and his sons have been 'through the mill' like the predecessors of the firm and are consummate connoisseurs of instruments and expert violin-makers, repairers and advisers. I speak from personal experience, having enjoyed the services of the house of W. E. Hill & Sons for some seventy years.

I have just seen a splendid viola made by Desmond Hill's father at the age of eighty-nine. It is a large viola with length of body 16¾ inches – even somewhat easier to manipulate than the Tertis Model. He is still making them at the age of ninety and there is every likelihood of his breaking the record of Stradivarius who made his last instrument at the age of ninety-three – for he can still bend and touch his toes!

It was with considerable pleasure that I recently heard that William Primrose had gone to Japan to preach the gospel of the solo viola there to a large number of enthusiastic Japanese embryo viola-players; he had been invited to teach for a year or more at the National University of Music and Fine Arts. He tells me that there is a Society of Japanese Violists which numbers several hundreds, mostly young men. He was informed that there are some good fiddle-makers in Japan and wanted to know where he could obtain the drawings and specifications of the T.M. viola. I was glad to be able to give him the name of the Japanese firm who market them in Japan. On my ninety-sixth birthday I received the following cable: 'Tokyo. Best wishes for the happiest of birthdays from William and Hiroko Primrose and students Hisatomi Sugimura Nakamura Fukui Tsuitsui Kunori Watanabe Nitanda Ejima Yamagisha and Shimazaki.'

17

Reflection

In expressing the wonderful efforts and success of humanity I am
confident universal opinion will agree with what I impatiently want
to affirm, namely that all human effort (even the fact of that astounding advance in technology, that we on earth are able to converse with
our fellow human beings walking on the moon) cannot be compared
to the miracles of nature; may I therefore record with all humility
the paramount thought that has ever guided and spurred me to try
and improve my humble and puny efforts in the interpretation of
music. In moments of human failing when one feels pride in one's
accomplishments, one has only to compare and contemplate the
unceasing wonders of nature to come down to earth with a jolt,
and as a result to realize the insignificance of our activities. This
reflection, throughout my life, has helped me to strive for betterment in my job. A colleague once accused me of trying to split hairs
in groping for Utopia. But why not? I see nothing against endeavour-
ing to attain the impossible, however inadequate our efforts may be
towards that goal.

I am grateful beyond words to have lived this long life of mine in
which I have been given the opportunity to help, in however small
a way, towards raising the status of a once neglected but lovely
instrument – the viola. It has been a long struggle, at times
grievously discouraging, at others greatly rewarding, and ever
completely absorbing.

For the String Player

The gratification of interpretative art lies in the fulfilment of its immense responsibilities.

L.T.

Beauty of Tone in String Playing

*I have read your treatise with great interest
and it seems to me that it constitutes a very
valuable contribution to the pedagogical
literature of our art.
Based on years of study and proven beyond doubt
by your own magnificent achievements, your
observations will carry great weight with
your colleagues and all students alike.*
Fritz Kreisler to the author

INTRODUCTION

This treatise is exclusively devoted to a *proved* method for acquiring expressive beauty of tone. It does not deal with the acrobatics of string playing.

I do not presume that the system here given is in any way a new discovery, or that it is the only course to pursue in order to extract from an inanimate string instrument a noble and poetic reflection of human sentiment. But I hold that if the following instructions are strictly adhered to, they will induce the string player to acquire expressive tone quality. I offer this opinion with confidence from the fact that my pupils have, without exception, gained beauty of tone and true expressiveness in following this method, which I have taught for seventy years or more.

I ask the reader to look upon these pages as a written lesson. I have freely *emphasized* important points to my invisible pupils, and *repeated* at times certain observations in order to ram them home. But I have endeavoured throughout to make my lesson as concise as possible.

I assume that the player has an instrument of passable good quality, correctly adjusted. There are many essentials, all of which are necessary to attain beauty of tone. The lack of any one of these will prevent the full realization of the power to extract from the instrument an ideally expressive sound, thrilling to the listener.

Under their separate headings I shall try to elucidate those essentials which in the light of my experience as a string player go to constitute this much-desired result.

THE LEFT HAND

Intonation

Perfect intonation is the rock-foundation of the string player's equipment. Without this absolute essential of essentials no one should be allowed to perform in public.

Faulty intonation in *most* cases is the result of utter carelessness, and is an unpardonable sin. It should be a *habit* to play in tune and not a habit to play out of tune.

Most of us who profess to play a string instrument have 'good ears', that is, sensitive to true intonation, and what is more, most of us are capable of discerning and attaining this. But how many do not!

A 'good ear' can become permanently perverted by negligent, superficial, non-penetrative listening on the part of the performer. This inattention to one's faculty of hearing is a vice of such rapid growth that in a very short time the player accepts faulty intonation with equanimity, eventually becoming quite unconscious that he is playing out of tune.

The certain road to never-failing perfect intonation is listening of the most *concentrated* kind. There is a vast difference between listening and listening *intently*. It is the latter which is absolutely imperative. The player must always be on the 'qui vive' and must never relax his listening faculties. The moment a note sounds in the slightest degree out of tune, *correct it immediately*. You will notice how much richer is the sound of a note that is *absolutely* in tune. A note infinitesimally flat or sharp lacks the rich, round, penetrative, luscious sound that only a note perfectly in tune will give you.

If you can attain perfect intonation – and you can – you are more than half-way on the road to real beauty of sound.

Whenever starting to practise a phrase, test the *first* note of it with an appropriate open string which will enable you to be sure that your starting note is in tune (assuming that your four strings are perfectly tuned). This comparison also applies of course to *any note* of which you are in doubt. I repeat with all the emphasis I can – the golden rule is to listen *intently* and *correct immediately*.

Vibrato

A supreme quality of vibrato is an indispensable element towards expressing your innermost feelings.

The vibrato to be cultivated is one that is neither too slow nor too fast. A too slow vibrato is an unhealthy sound, producing a sentimental effect. It is positively sick-making. A too fast vibrato militates against serenity and is nervously irritating to say the least of it. Avoid them both and so achieve a happy medium.

I do not suggest that there is any absolute method for acquiring the perfect vibrato, we are all built differently. You must practise until you obtain the feeling of the satisfactory degree of pulsation. The only method I venture to propose is to put your finger hard on the string and oscillate it infinitesimally from side to side until you obtain what you consider is the right pace of vibrato. The vital factor about vibrato is that it should be continuous; there must be no break in it whatsoever, especially at the moment of proceeding from one note to another, whether those notes are in the same position or whether a change of position is involved. The vibrato in the note you are playing must start at the very beginning of that note (or possibly infinitesimally before the bow touches the string) – and must join the following note without stopping. In other words, KEEP YOUR FINGERS ALIVE! A phrase is spoilt by allowing them momentarily to go dead, i.e. by the cessation of the vibrato. Let me explain what I mean in a slightly different way: if the finger momentarily ceases to oscillate at the end of the note you are playing, the sound becomes dead, and *more so* if the note following it is not immediately alive for the first split second that the finger contacts the string.

An otherwise beautifully played slow or cantabile phrase in which an open string occurs is often marred by the player's failure to do anything to counteract the dead tone of the open string when he arrives at it. Tone quality can be given to it (providing you are *obliged* to use an open string) by sympathetic vibration on a stopped note on another string (not of course touched by the bow) either an octave, or some other appropriate interval, above or below; or by putting the finger *behind* the nut of the fingerboard of the open string – if there is time for so doing. The unison when available is very effective. The occasions are rare indeed when the blatant tone of the open string is specifically required.

The momentary stopping of the vibrato, all too prevalent among string players, and the cause of ruining expressive tone quality of a phrase, is particularly likely to occur in changing positions. It should never occur. KEEP YOUR FINGERS ALIVE! I repeat – there is nothing so deadly or ruinous to an expressive phrase as the sound of a cantabile slow passage in which one or two notes are partly or wholly devoid of vibrato.

A continuous vibrato (in other words life in the fingers), properly used not abused, affords the essence of beauty of tone and expression. It must be of correct pace under all conditions. Nothing is so hateful as an unnatural, overdone and insincere vibrato. If you possess the true kind of expressive feeling within yourself you will soon find what is the correct pace of vibrato for all occasions. Indeed this will – it can only – come *naturally*.

It should be noted that vibrato properly executed is a very decisive factor in the enhancement of resonance and carrying power of the instrument.

I ask the reader once again to excuse my frequent reiteration of instructions, but I feel it is of extreme importance in the case of a written lesson such as this.

Portamento

Portamento is another resource which, unless employed with the utmost discretion, can ruin the artistry of string playing. Incorrectly performed, or overdone in the slightest degree, it can make all the difference between sentiment and that horrid word 'sentimentality', the latter in this case resulting in abominable vulgarity.

Portamento is the means of joining or linking two notes of varied distances between them, smoothly and naturally. It is *not* a discernible slide; it is an infinitesimal join. The art of its use is to avoid break, jerk or nauseous slide. It is a most necessary adjunct to legato playing and can either enhance or mar beauty of expression. A more or less general rule to be observed in the application of portamento is that, if employed between two notes *in the same bow*, the finger that is on the string operates the discreet (or short) slide, not the finger that is off the string (which represents the note to be approached) – and generally in the case of portamento between two notes, *each note having a separate bow*, the finger that is off the string generally does the sliding. In the latter case an infinitesimal and hardly discernible slide is all that should take place; just before the second note. In the former case, however (that is, two notes in the same bow), the finger that is on the string slides almost into the relative position applicable to the second note, and is then taken off like greased lightning at the moment of playing the second note. The celerity with which this is done is the secret of discreet natural portamento. Always be discreet.

There must be no drawling, languishing or lingering in the action of the slide. Keep the fingers *judiciously* alive during the process of the portamento. The vibrato must be continuous in the finger on the string, and the second note must absolutely join this vibrato, an observation of importance towards our goal of beauty of tone. Unless portamento is accomplished in the many ways I have described, the fulfilment of perfect portamento will not be achieved, and the expressiveness of your emotions will be marred.

Portamento, then, is a device used for dovetailing the distance between two notes which are not in the same position, be the notes a short or long distance apart. It must *never* be employed from a note into an open string – a more unhealthy sound could not be imagined.

THE RIGHT HAND

Practise to develop equality of tone with the bow. You must try to get as much tone from the point of the bow as you are able to do at the heel – i.e. throughout the whole length of the bow. To achieve this, draw the bow across the string fortissimo as slowly as possible, without any suspicion of scrape or scratch, the tone being *equal throughout the whole length of the bow*. In the same manner, practise long, slow bows pianissimo. There must be no sign of dither, crescendo or diminuendo in either case. Subtleties of phrasing and expression such as crescendo, diminuendo, accented notes, etc., must also be practised. But for equal volume of tone, the long, concentrated slow bow is the method to pursue. It is most important to develop to a high state of perfection this equality of tone, so essential to smooth or legato playing.

Another vital necessity is to obtain this smoothness, evenness and continuity of sound at the actual moment of bowing from one string to another. While playing on the one string you must, in preparation for crossing, get your bow as near as you dare to the string you are about to play upon; indeed the art lies in drawing the bow from one string to another with the crossing-over remaining absolutely imperceptible. The ideal is to convey the impression that your instrument has one string only, not four. A further valuable acquirement for legato playing is to make your bow belong, so to speak, to the string. The bow should literally cling to it. The ethereal sound of a passage played pianissimo by a *slow* clinging bow can be exquisite.

Again, a necessity of the highest importance is to *keep your* (left hand) *fingers alive*, especially at the moment of crossing the strings. To be more explicit, the finger must remain and vibrate on the string you are about to leave until you have actually begun to play the note on the next string – and this second note must immediately take up the vibrato of the note you are just leaving.

I emphasize and repeat: KEEP YOUR FINGERS ALIVE. They must not go dead; the vibrato must not stop for the slightest fraction of a second. For evenness and continuity of sound, the importance of this cannot be overestimated. But never forget – the vibrato must be discreet and not overdone.

Another very necessary attainment is to conceal the changing of the bow from down to up, or vice versa. There must be no sign of jerk or break; indeed it must sound as if the arm and bow were of unlimited length and never had to change, unless of course accents or any other effects are indicated. Quantity of tone is not produced by brute force of pressure of the bow on the string; on the contrary, the result of this is a harsh and coarse sound, with considerable reduction of carrying power. Over-pressure of the bow chokes the instrument. You must find out the limit of pressure applicable to the particular instrument you are using, and not exceed it. Screw your bow up tightly enough so that the bow hair does not touch the stick under pressure. How often does one hear the wood of the bow hit the strings, especially in spiccato playing – much to the detriment of the clarity of the sound.

One can obtain a delightful subtlety of expression (a quite ethereal sound) in pianissimo playing if one uses the bow *very slowly* and *very little* of it, at the point of the bow.

Many other types of expression are produced by bow technique, such as the détaché bow, the martelé, staccato, spiccato, ricochet, etc. But I am not dealing with acrobatics of the right or left hand.

The subject to which I am confining myself is a specialized method for producing expressive singing tone.

The shape of the bridge has an important relation to equality of tone. The arch must not be too convex or too flat. And remember that any one string which is microscopically too high or too low will land both your hands in difficulties, either for clearance of the string, or for ease in double or triple stopping.

CANTABILE PLAYING IN THE ORCHESTRA

The lack of expressiveness in the string section – why is it? My argument is that we could have more warmth of tone in all the orchestras I have ever heard. I am *convinced* I know an important factor for this unnecessary lack of expression.

I would like to suggest that if we heard the players individually in a melodic phrase, a good measure of expressive playing would be forthcoming, but when these players are heard collectively quite a good deal of this expressiveness disappears, and the sounds at times are almost phlegmatic. It is the few who have either a too-quick or too-slow vibrato who spoil the ship for a ha'p'orth of tar. The suggestions put forward in this treatise I feel might help to make good this deficiency in sensitivity, or coldness in collective playing, that we so often hear.

It is detrimental to expressiveness if part of the section play a melodic phrase on one string, while others in the same section employ two strings for the same phrase, i.e., unanimity of fingering and choice of position is essential.

Another important point in expressive playing is the failure to execute portamenti in the correct manner. See the appropriate section of this treatise.

MEMORANDA

The string instrument is capable of unlimited shades of expression. Study them.

Understand and make the difference apparent between piano and pianissimo.

Ensure that there is a positive distinction between mezzoforte, forte and fortissimo.

The words crescendo and decrescendo mean increasing and decreasing the tone *gradually*. They do not mean *sudden* loudness or softness. Remember that in pianissimo playing you must also use all the intensity of feeling you have within you to express your emotions. It is more difficult to do so when playing pianissimo than when playing forte.

Probe into, using your musicality to the utmost, tone gradation, accents, rhythm, or even alteration of phrasing, etc., all of which will relieve monotony and lend colour and expressiveness to your efforts. Do not feel absolutely *bound* to abide by *all* the printed nuances you find in the work you are playing. An alteration here and there that really appeals to you is not a crime and will provide a change from other interpretations and show your own individuality.

Variety of fingering is another factor making for expressive tone-quality, especially when two identical passages immediately follow one another. Whenever possible use a different string for the repetition of a phrase – for the sake of the altered colour and general vitality of effect which the variation in the method employed affords. If this is not possible and the repetition can only be played on the same string, use all your ingenuity to give the repetition as much alteration of fingering as you can, for the important effect of variety.

In playing pizzicato do not allow the fingernail to contact the string, and/or the string to rebound on the fingerboard with the resultant clatter. Hans Richter once stopped his orchestra and addressed the violin section, who were playing a phrase pizzicato, as follows: 'Nicht mit die nagel – mit die "meat".' ('Not with the nail – with the flesh.')

In playing pizzicato chords double forte on violin or viola, hit – don't pick – your four strings with your second finger from the A string to the C string, *not* from the C string to the A string. If you hit the strings from the C to the A, the strings will contact the fingerboard with consequent objectionable clatter; whereas if you *hit* them from the A to the C string, i.e. obliquely upwards to the C string, no matter how fortissimo, there will be no resultant clatter. (This applies to wire strings. See my comments on the use of wire strings for the viola under *Maintenance of your instrument*.)

When playing a string instrument, obliterate from your mind the fact that you are making music out of such crude materials as wood, hair, resin, strings. The goal to work for is the feeling that the sounds brought into being are an expression of yourself. The instrument and bow in your imagination should be non-existent. It is no mere fancy but a fact of experience that by this means one does in some measure obviate those superficial noises arising from contact of bow and string, so detrimental and disturbing to purity of sound.

Most performers at some time or other during their professional careers are particularly prone to suffer from neuritis, fibrositis or other itises through ignorance of the science of anatomy as it affects them. Teachers of string players should emphasize the importance of *correct stance*. The soloist who has to stand to practise or perform in public should put equal weight on both feet, and not, as is more usual, put most of the weight on the left foot, resulting eventually in curvature of the spine, etc. Exercise and massage are also vitally necessary, particularly if the executant indulges, as he should, in practice, *practice* and PRACTICE.

Long hair and locks over the right or left eyebrow are nauseating to look at and utterly useless in furthering musical capability.

Maintenance of your instrument

The use of resin is generally overdone. Very little is sufficient. Keep your instrument clean, especially the fingerboard and neck. If you use metal strings (I never use any other for the simple reason that I consider wire strings give better results for the *viola* than gut), clean them *occasionally* with some such spirit as Eau-de-Cologne. When using resin, clean it off with a dry cloth – downward strokes. Never allow the resin to get thick and clogged. The spirit must be used *very* sparingly and with extreme care, for if it touches the varnish it will bring it off. In cleaning the strings, clean the fingerboard at the same time and you will be surprised to find how dirty it is. Do not touch the neck (back of fingerboard) with the spirit – it can be cleaned with a very slightly damp piece of cloth. As for cleaning the body of the instrument I have always found W. E. Hill's Cleaner the most satisfactory.

If you use gut strings, choose only the best and of correct thickness for your instrument. An incorrect gauge of string is detrimental to tone.

See that your pegs fit properly. If they become too tight or too loose they can generally be made to work smoothly by applying a little Peg Compound. In an emergency, use dry soap, followed by a little chalk. If this proves unsuccessful, go to the repairer.

If wire strings are used, see that the tuners of the tailpiece are taut, without any suspicion of loose parts – the cause of many an annoying rattle, sometimes difficult to diagnose.

Make sure that your strings are *equally and most accurately* spaced at the nut (top of the fingerboard) and on the bridge. You must experiment as to whether the spacing should be wider or narrower.

Adjustments to your instrument should be carried out only by an expert violin-maker.

It is important that your strings should be at the correct height from the fingerboard. Because the viola is in the middle register, metal strings make it a quicker-speaking instrument. A point to look at is that wire strings, having more tension than gut strings, should be adjusted so as to be as near to the fingerboard as possible – of course *without* any sign of rattle when played upon.

Having come to the conclusion in my early days of playing the viola that metal strings are preferable to gut for this instrument, I brought out what I called the 'Tertis' bridge cushion, which not only resists indentation and widening of the nitches on the bridge, but also enables the player to raise any string an accurate $\frac{1}{32}$ or $\frac{1}{64}$ of an inch. This bridge protector is narrow at the point of contact with the bridge and has an aperture through which the string can be threaded. It is marketed by British Music and Tennis Strings Ltd, and any royalties therefrom are donated to the Musicians' Benevolent Fund.

YOURSELF

The way to attain intensity of expression

Does it not stand to reason that to bring to life a viola, violin, cello or double bass (all of which are inanimate lumps of wood with appendages), in order to reproduce the emotional sensibility of which you are capable, you must bring into force all the vitality your body and soul possess?

You must play and interpret with the utmost intensity of feeling, be it fortissimo or pianissimo, appassionata or cantabile, all the time and every time. In no other way can the inert instrument be brought fully to life and made to transmit the reality of your sentiments; but above all, understand the difference between sentiment and senti- ' mentality – and avoid the latter like the plague.

Do not forget that your playing will reflect your innermost self. Therefore, to make your power of expression worth listening to, it is necessary to mould your mind and action through life to all that is of the utmost sincerity.

The interpreter of music in its highest form must rise in his music-making above the levels of the everyday world, its commonness and its vanity, and hold himself apart, in an atmosphere of idealism.

I repeat my maxim quoted at the beginning of this section of the book: 'The gratification of interpretative art lies in the fulfilment of its immense responsibilities.' Added to which I say with all the vehemence and certainty I can muster: the result will be the enhancement of your quality of tone production.

The Art of String Quartet Playing*

*To the memory of my dear friend Richard Capell
who championed the cause of the viola as a solo
instrument at any and every opportunity. With
gratitude, I dedicate this treatise to him.*
L.T.

I hope I may be pardoned for 'blowing my own trumpet' sotto voce in asserting the reason for deeming myself worthy of expressing my convictions on this most important subject of musical interpretation. It lies in the fact of my experience of playing in very many quartet and other small ensembles, and also in my years of teaching the art of string quartet playing. The hints and opinions I shall put forward are addressed not only to the budding string quartet ensemble, but also, with due respect, in part to professional quartets in full bloom.

First, the following are the absolute prerequisites of a high standard of quartet playing.

Great technical capability, together with fine musicianship on the part of all four players, is an absolute necessity. Less obvious, and often utterly disregarded, is the next essential – a close relation in tone quality between the four instruments themselves. This very important factor is more difficult to achieve than the layman would suppose. And still more important and hard to attain is the next vital requisite – the players must agree. Their dispositions must exclude any semblance of so-called dignity, they must be at one in musicianship and outlook. The way of perfection is beset with pitfalls. Very frequently a fine combination has disintegrated through petty quarrels. And it is very often the case that one hears an ensemble ruined by the lack of warmth of expression in the playing of one or another of the members.

The leader of the professional quartet needs to be a master musician and a virtuoso, with a mind of profound musical under-

* Most of what is said here also applies to playing in other small ensembles.

standing and hands adequate to cope with the library of scores bristling with most formidable technical difficulties. Herein is a great obstacle in the way of perfection because the violinists of this calibre are few who are ready to divide modest spoils into four equal parts. Let the listener who hears such a one realize that that violinist could do much better for himself, financially, by solo playing.

A supremely fine string quartet of players must necessarily have high ideals which entail sacrifices, and it follows therefore in such a case, that they should have, and are entitled to, some measure of subsidy. My mind goes back to the various teams I have heard and I give the palm to the Curtis Quartet; as I felt when they gave a concert in the Aeolian Hall, London, very many years ago, they touched the ideal. They were subsidized by the Curtis Institute of Philadelphia. They had all the attributes one could possibly hope for: warmth of expression, technical ability, and the all-important requisite – fine musicianship.

How hard to come by is the team spirit. And yet without it, all chamber music is vanity. Self-conceit and a sense of superiority on the part of any one of the members and the spirit has fled, damnation sets in. To the right frame of mind must be added intense and incessant application. It is a hard road.

Having laid down the paramount necessities for the ideal string quartet I will enumerate hints that I have found from experience helpful towards realizing this highest form of interpretation in music.

1. A fine ensemble can only be achieved by specialization. To obtain a good balance of tone, cultivate the habit of listening separately as it were, to yourself, and at the same time to your colleagues.

2. Practise together very long slow bows pianissimo from heel to point of bow, and from point to heel.

3. In the same manner practise very long slow bows fortissimo for the full length of the bow, as slowly as possible without scraping or forcing the tone.

4. Again practise starting together in pianissimo and fortissimo at different parts of the bow. The start must be absolutely simultaneous without the suspicion of preliminary sound or dither; in other words the fact that the bow exists must be entirely effaced.

5. Practise also starting together with bows on the string and off the string.

6. The players should arrange their bowings so that absolute

unanimity in phrasing including up and down bows is attained where possible.

7. Alertness should be practised in rehearsal. For example, from time to time the leader should alter, without notice to his colleagues, the established tempo, nuance, etc. to test the alertness of the others in falling in with his departure. It may well happen in an actual concert performance that one member or another could, in the heat of the moment, vary the tempo or nuance previously agreed upon, and in an alert quartet the others will conform without the quiver of an eyelid.

8. Tune your instrument most accurately before going on to the platform – you will achieve a more exact tuning if *each* player first obtains the A most meticulously from the leader, and then tunes his or her instrument separately. With regard to the tuning of the viola and cello, it should be an added safeguard if these players after tuning their instruments compare their C strings, because the pitch of their instruments being an octave apart, there is the greater difficulty in obtaining absolute accuracy. If the C strings do not agree, then manifestly the tuning has not been done sufficiently carefully. As I have said in 'Beauty of Tone' listen *intently*.

9. Avoid tuning on the platform as far as possible. There is nothing so distressing or disturbing to the continuity of the work as tuning one's instrument between movements. If tune you must, put your instrument to your ear and pizzicato with your left hand pianissimo (audible only to your own ear).

10. Avoid open strings unless a blatant sound is actually wanted. The open string is generally an undesirable intruder.

11. Members should practise their individual parts with utter scrupulousness and overcome all technical difficulties before attending rehearsal. Each should be able to play his part standing on his head, so to speak!

12. Above all, never lose sight of the fact that if the lump of wood that is under your chin or between your knees is to yield a living expressive utterance of your emotional feeling, you must throw yourself, heart and soul and all that you are, into the adventure. Make the sounds you produce, whether in fortissimo or pianissimo, the expression of your innermost self. (I have said this in *Beauty of Tone*, but I repeat it here because of its importance.)

13. Each music stand should be adjusted to as low a position as possible so that each player has a full view of the others. At the same

time the four players should arrange to *face* the audience as much as is feasible, and not sit in the orthodox square position, because this prevents the full volume of their tone capacity from reaching the auditorium. (On this point see Chapter 15, on my orchestral seating plan.)

14. Do not resort to obvious gestures in order to make a simultaneous start. Two winks from the leader, unseen by the audience, will give the tempo and in most cases should be sufficient.

15. Distinguish most scrupulously between piano and pianissimo, forte and fortissimo, and see to it that in crescendo and diminuendo, the swell and diminution of sound are precisely the same on all four instruments as the phrase begins and ends.

16. When you have exact or repetitive phrases, especially when they immediately follow one another, difference of fingering and change of string if possible for each phrase is an important factor because it adds variety and colour to your expressive efforts.

17. In the case of crescendo or diminuendo, accelerando or rallentando the alteration in quantity of tone or change of tempo should be so gradually and imperceptibly performed that the effect becomes a natural one and the listener will be unaware of how it has been arrived at.

I address the following observations to the pianist when joining in performance with the string quartet, trio, or other small ensemble.

1. Let not your piano lid be fully open. Use the short stick. The strings can very rarely cope with all the volume of tone that your massive instrument is capable of. Endeavour always to keep a balance between your tone and the strings'.

2. Be on your guard especially with your left hand. The ponderous bass of the piano can so easily overwhelm the strings.

3. Be cautious in the use of the pedals, and, of great importance, be careful with the sustaining pedal.

4. It is a habit among many pianists, when they have a melodic phrase to interpret, to dig into the keys of what is after all – and I say it without apology – practically a mechanical instrument, in the supposition that they are being expressive. The result is not the intended one. On the contrary, the fingers should crawl over and literally caress the keys in such phrases, if the pianist is to get anywhere near the string players' great asset – that is, being able to

express his innermost emotions through the use of his left-hand vibrato and right-hand bow technique.

5. When the pianoforte combines with the string quartet, listen most intently. Be on the qui vive at all times to hear the other players *as well as yourself.*

May I stress – take note of all these directions which have emanated from practical experience. It is only on the rarest occasion that one hears a satisfying balance of tone where the piano is concerned in small ensembles.

Having laid down what I feel is necessary for the attainment of the ideal string quartet combination or other small ensemble, I should like to emphasize that I have done so in no spirit of dictatorship to my fellow-musicians, but in the hope that the suggestions I have made both in this essay and in that on Beauty of Tone will prove of use to them in what is surely the highest form of music interpretation.

Hints to Composers*

Some sixty years ago when I first began to play the viola as a solo instrument in earnest, I was sitting next to a lady at a dinner party when she suddenly fired a question at me: 'What is a *voila*?' Recovering from this surprising onslaught, and being a well-behaved youth of twenty, I proceeded to explain to her what it was, and that it was not spelt V-O-I-L-A, but V-I-O-L-A, and pronounced VEEOLA. I also recall, at one of the first concerts I ever played at as a soloist, overhearing someone remark to his neighbour: 'I believe a viola is a peculiarly-shaped brass instrument'! Such was the singular situation that viola soloists were up against as recently as 1896.

There were only one or two of us preaching the gospel in those days; now we have an army of good viola-players all over the globe. Increasing numbers of violinists are taking it up, and I am confident this movement will go on. They find they are in much greater request as violists. There are many good violinists, but not enough good viola-players, and let me say further to the violinist, that once you become a viola-player one of your most important duties is to strive to enlarge the library of solo viola music, by fair means or foul. Cajole your composer friends to write for it, raid the repertory of the violin, cello or any other instrument, and arrange and transcribe works from their literature suitable for your viola. The Pecksniffian attitude that it is sacrilege to transpose works from the original to another medium is fast disappearing. I have never had a qualm about making arrangements myself, providing of course that they sound well on the viola. My conscience in this matter remains one of sublime righteousness. On the contrary I consider it a pious act to grab music for the viola, and further, my urge to add to the library of viola music has always been strengthened by the fact that

---

* The substance of a paper I read for the Composers' Concourse on 2 December 1954 at the instigation of Sir William Glock.

the great masters themselves rearranged no end of their works, for all sorts of instruments and combinations.

May I suggest that present-day composers could spare a little of their creative talent for the ex-Cinderella? They would earn the eternal gratitude of viola-players present and future, providing of course their work was written for the viola and not against it! I mean by that, *do* let us have a tune in it occasionally – especially on the C string which after all is the characteristic quality of the viola. I hope this plea will not be a cry in the wilderness. I do feel there is quite enough world discordance without adding to it with jarring dissonance, which is so prevalent and overdone. What are the causes of these inflictions? Is it due to the frantic pace of life which seems to become faster and faster? Whatever walk of life one is concerned with, one has the impression of being poked in the middle of the back by someone with a long pole and remorselessly pushed by it from morning till bed-time – not very conducive to inspiration and beauty! The very nature of music demands that it should not be entirely abstract, and should contain something which will appeal to the listener's emotions. The viola is in its element in melodious phrases. Its tone quality is very human in character.

Now, may I with diffidence make one or two suggestions to all composers with regard to the employment of the solo viola with orchestra. The viola's particular character of tone being in the middle register, it is necessary that the orchestration should not be too heavy when accompanying. I remember in my early days playing the Benjamin Dale Suite for viola and full orchestra (which was originally written for viola and piano), the scoring of which is as follows: in addition to some sixty string players, there are two flutes, two oboes, cor anglais, three clarinets, bass clarinet, bassoon, four horns, two trumpets, three trombones, tuba, timpani, every known species of percussion, celesta, and two harps – that's all! Hans Richter was conducting it and I recall that he complained to me, after the rehearsal, of the huge orchestra employed, saying: 'I suppose the next addition they will find necessary for accompanying the poor dear viola will be a battery of exploding air-balloons!'

As an example of most satisfactory use of sparse orchestral material, take Mozart's Sinfonia Concertante for violin, viola and orchestra which is scored for strings, two oboes, two horns, and nothing more. How satisfying and complete it all is – never are the solo instruments blotted out. I don't mean to suggest that all works should or could be so orchestrated, moreover there is no reason why the orchestra should not blaze away to its heart's content with all its kitchen utensils in the tuttis, but when the soloist has something to say, for heaven's sake give him a chance to say it.

I would suggest the cutting down of the strings, at all times when the solo viola is playing, to say three desks of first violins, three desks of second violins, no violas, two desks of cellos, and one desk of basses – for the strings are generally inconsiderate, unwilling or incapable of accompanying softly enough. Apparently the strings don't realize that with fifty or sixty of them playing at one and the same time, they ought to use only one hair of the bow, so to speak, when accompanying. If I were fortunate enough to be a composer, and if I were writing for viola and orchestra, I should omit the viola section from the score, in order to allow the solo viola to stand alone and avoid detraction from its tone colour by a similar quality of sound in the orchestra. I would also suggest omitting clarinets, because I have found that their tone quality in their thick middle register seems to rob and clash with that of the viola. A rather nice effect would be the viola and harp alone at times, as at the beginning of Berlioz's *Harold in Italy*. Also, a neglected medium is the viola as obbligato to the voice; here, because of its middle register, it is better than the violin or cello.

The Tertis Model Viola*

The design of the violas to which you are listening today has been conceived, first as a result of the scarcity of violas, and secondly, because of the deficiencies of small, and the difficulties of impossibly large violas still in circulation. These drawbacks and obstacles have continually confronted me during my fifty-seven years of viola playing. The small violas have insufficient air-space and therefore lack C string sonority. The large ones of 17 or 18 inches in length, with their cumbersome features, effectively prevent ease of manipulation. As my colleague William Primrose once pungently remarked with regard to the very large viola: 'The viola is difficult enough without having to indulge in a wrestling match with it!'

The many different sizes of violas in circulation make it difficult for a player to go from one instrument to another (as is possible with the more or less standardized violin), and it is this lack of standardization also in the viola which we are trying to rectify and which has hitherto been an obstacle to its progress. Now that the viola has obtained and is consolidating its rightful place on the musical map, more than ever necessary is the provision of good instruments, of which there is a great scarcity the world over. There is nothing like enough for the growing army of efficient and discerning viola-players.

The 'Tertis Model' will help to correct these shortages and defects. It is $16\frac{3}{4}$ inches long, and this I consider to be the maximum length for playing under the chin, and, at the same time, the minimum from which to hope for a really satisfactory C string sonority. I was encouraged to find that Alfred Hill – that great connoisseur of string instruments and son of William E. Hill (founder of the famous house of violin- and bow-makers in New Bond Street) – agreed with me that this was the correct size for the ideal viola.

* Lecture I gave at the Wigmore Hall on 4 December 1950.

In the Tertis Model we have been fortunate in our arrangement of air-space; and also incorporated are other features, resulting from my practical experience, which make it, for its size, easy to handle. The fact that since 1938 approximately a hundred and thirty of these violas have been made [as at 1950], mostly by eminent professional craftsmen, here and in other countries, and that the vast majority of these instruments are in the hands of professional viola-players, speaks for itself. The standardization of the viola for which I am striving, though as yet by no means achieved, is well on the way and, I think, will prove to have a most beneficent influence in furthering the cause of the viola.

I should like to pay tribute to the violin-maker Arthur Richardson. I am particularly indebted to him for the many experiments which he made towards realizing my theories with regard to the ideal viola from the player's point of view, and I venture to suggest our collaboration has not been in vain. Mr Richardson enjoyed the unique distinction of being the first man in the history of fiddle craftsmanship to have made nearly one hundred violas [to date – 1950], to be precise, ninety-seven. I want also to thank Mr C. Lovett Gill, eminent architect and amateur violin-maker, for his fine drawing of the design of this instrument. These drawings are in use in many parts of the globe. Mr Gill has made seven of these violas, one of which you have heard today.

On my own behalf may I add that neither in the viola nor the scheme have I any financial interest whatsoever. Not a few of my friends have accused me of being an altruistic duffer in not accepting financial reward for my part in the development of this viola, and for distributing the drawings and specifications to violin craftsmen, in the early days, free of charge. But if I had, this would have sent up the price of the instrument; and we viola-players as a class have never been and, I fear, never will be particularly affluent. Further, I would not have my endeavours for the viola in this direction tainted with monetary gain. My satisfaction lies in the fact that I have helped to provide the present and future generation of viola-players with a fine-toned and manageable instrument.

From the very beginning of my campaign for the viola in 1896 I have found that anything, however slightly unorthodox, that tends towards progress has generally met with violent opposition, and I know that some craftsmen and violin dealers resent the idea that a mere instrumentalist should dare to lay down the law as to the design of the viola. But I have had much experience of being up against prejudice, and am deaf to insignificant opposition. I know that I am not a violin-maker, nor am I a scientist, nor do I understand the secrets of acoustics. Who does? But I say to violin-makers that I have kept my eyes and ears open for nearly half a century and have put two and two together. In other words, the design is simply an amalgamation of all the good points of the old masters in the many instruments I have seen, heard and played, plus anything I have learned that makes for ease in manipulating the larger dimensions of the viola.

APPENDIX

Violin Craftsmen Who Make the Tertis Model Viola

In 1965 there were over six hundred Tertis Model violas in existence, played mostly by professional viola-players. The drawings and specifications are now available to amateur as well as professional craftsmen and may be purchased from the sole distributors Messrs W. E. Hill & Sons, 140 New Bond Street, London, W.1. Profits from the sale of these drawings are donated to the Royal Society of Musicians Samaritan Fund.

Tertis Model instruments (as I write in 1973) are made in these seventeen countries: Argentina, Australia, Bulgaria, Canada, Czechoslovakia, Denmark, Finland, France, Germany, Great Britain, Holland, Italy, Japan, Spain, Switzerland, United States and Venezuela. In order to assist viola-players who may be in search of a T.M. instrument, I here give the addresses of some violin craftsmen who make them, in as much detail as I have been able to ascertain. Many of the addresses, however, date from 1965. The list does not include twenty-nine craftsmen of various countries who did not vouchsafe a reply to my request of 1965 for information as to the number of T.M. violas they had built.

Argentina	Emilio Petraglia, Pichenta 403, 2-B, Buenos Aires
Australia	William Dolphin, 272 Bourke St, Melbourne Norman Miller, Box 33, City North, Toowoomba, Queensland
Bulgaria	Ivan Kaloferov, Conservatoire d'Etat de Sofia, Boul. kl. Gotwald 11
Canada	E. Charlton, 56 Queen Anne Rd, Toronto, Ontario S. Engen, Box 610, Dauphin, Manitoba George Friess, 2724 Yale St, Vancouver, British Columbia Joseph Reid, R.R. 2, Grimsby, Ontario
Czechoslovakia	Otaka Spidlen, Prague 2, Gottwadlove nabr. 12 Karel Vavra, Korunni Trida 28, Prague 2
Denmark	Emil Hjorth, Ny Vestergade 1, Copenhagen Knud Vestergaard, 61 Oester Alle, Viby J.

Finland	Jukka Bergman, Fabianinkatu 27 B, Helsinki
	Risto Vaimo, Krakallie, Kilo, Helsinki (introd. by Jan Sedenholm, Finnish Radio Orchestra, Alexandersgatan 36, Helsingfors)
France	Jean Bauer, 34 Rue Rabelais, Angers
	Etienne Vatelot, 11 rue Portalis, Paris 75008
Germany (West)	Walter Feiler, Radiumbad, Brambach, Saxony (Forst 166)
	Horner, Schonbacherstrasse 17, Butenreuth, Co. Erlangen
	Karl Roy, Riedscharteweg 2, Mittenwald 8102
Great Britain	Maurice Bouette, Newark Technical College, Chauntry Park, Newark-on-Trent, Nottinghamshire
	Lawrance Cocker, 16 North Parade, Derby
	Sydney Evans (Paul Roth maker), 49 Berkley St, Birmingham, B1 2LG
	Arthur Richardson, Crediton, Devon
	W. Saunders, Nottingham
	Paul Voigt, 2 Gerrard Place, London W1.
Holland	Max Moller, Willemsparkweg 15, Amsterdam-Z
Italy	G. & L. Leandro Bisiach, Jr, Corse, Magenta 27, Milan
	Marino Capichioni, Rimini Viale, V. Veneto (T.M. quartets played by Carmirelli of Rome and Prof. Schanitt Quartets)
	Alberto Mingo, Via Sara Levi Nathan 14, Pessaro
Japan	Maruichi-Shoten, 27 Koraibashi 1 – Chame, Higashika, Osaka
Spain	Ignacio Fleta, Barcelona
Switzerland	Pierre Vidoudez, 22 Corraterie, Geneva
United States	F. Artindale, 1243 Palm St, San Luis Obispo, California Ausmus, California
	Martin Beilke, 3311 Newton Ave N., Minneapolis, Minnesota
	Elihu Boroson, 995 Hope St, Springdale, Connecticut
	Olav Breivik, 2449 N. Downer St, Milwaukee, Wisconsin
	H. R. Brown, 7002 Westmoreland Ave, Takoma Park, Maryland

United States
(*continued*)

Ed Chamberlain, Alton, New Hampshire
J. C. Cordell, 150 S. Bull St, Columbia, South
Carolina (T.M. string quartet of instruments)
F. R. Davidson, 137 E. Main St, Leipsic, Ohio
L. B. Davis, 5 Sharon Dr, Whippany, New Jersey
Lawrence Drake, 2920 River Rd, Eugene, Oregon
Joseph Franko, 95 Van Riper Ave, Clifton, New Jersey
Paul Franusich, Route 1, Box 1236, Elk Grove,
California
Frank Gelber, 5907 Fourth Ave, Vienna, North
Virginia
Ervin Hartzell, 3002 W. Farmington Rd, Peoria,
Illinois
E. W. Huntington, 1560 Picardy Dr, Stockton,
California
Jay Jamison, Penalosa, Kansas
F. Kahler, 832 N. Edison St, Arlington, Virginia
Adolph Kortegast, 103 Boulevard, Pelham, New York
Dr F. L. Laffoon, 869 Alta Vista Dr, Vista, California
Henry Lanini, 3414 Alum Roch Ave, San José,
California
Victor Lomax, 454 Norway Ave, Huntington, West
Virginia
Lee McNeese, Buffalo, Wyoming
Raymond Marsh, 510 W. Berry St, Ft Wayne, Indiana
Lothar Meisel, Highway 14 East, Owatouna,
Minnesota
Oscar Meissner, 5216 Rivoli Dr, Macon, Georgia
Meyers-Halvarson Co, Nashville, Michigan
William Moennig, 2039 Lucust St, Philadelphia,
Pennsylvania 19103
Nielsen Violin Shop, 1905 Harney St, Omaha,
Nebraska
W. C. Palmer, Postal Building 510, S.W. Third Ave,
Portland, Oregon
J. Rashid, 27620 Eldena Dr, San Pedro, California
Dudley Reed, Box 2815, University Station, Gains-
ville, Florida
D. C. Renno, Rm 418, 581 Dekalb Bend, Oregon
David Saunders, 405 West Galer St, Seattle,
Washington

United States
(*continued*)

W. E. Slaby, 1322 N. Vermont, Royal Oak, Michigan
Jacob Theodore, 238 E. 80th St, New York
Vladik Tkac, 422 Cass Ave, San Antonio, Texas
Frank Topolewsky, 1150 Belmont Ave, Toledo, Ohio
Charles Vermilyea, Rt 2, Box 476, Peoria, Arizona
R. Wallace, P.O. Box 367, Gilbert, Arizona
Joseph Walter, 1 Clinton Ave, Montclair, New Jersey
Ernest Wild, 14 Foss Ave, San Anselmo, California
Anthony Wrona, 980 Maryvale Dr, Buffalo, New York
Curt Wunderlich, 16641 E. Warren St, Detroit,
     Michigan

Works for Viola Solo

written for the author or arranged and edited for the viola by the author

PUBLISHED WORKS*

Works written for viola and orchestra

ARNOLD BAX. *Phantasy* (Concerto) (Murdoch)
T. F. DUNHILL. *Triptych* (Oxford University Press)
GUSTAV HOLST. *Lyric Movement* (Oxford University Press)
MOZART. Sinfonia Concertante in E flat (K. 364) for violin and viola, with a cadenza by L. T. (Oxford University Press)
W. H. REED. Rhapsody (Galliard)
RALPH VAUGHAN WILLIAMS. *Flos Campi*, for viola, orchestra and choir (Oxford University Press); Suite (Oxford University Press)
WILLIAM WALTON. Concerto (Oxford University Press)

Works written for viola and piano, etc.

ARNOLD BAX. Fantasy-Sonata for viola and harp (Murdoch); *Legend* (Murdoch); Sonata (Murdoch); Elegiac Trio for flute, viola and harp (Chester)
ARTHUR BLISS. Sonata (Oxford University Press)
YORK BOWEN. Sonatas in C minor and F (Schott); Melodies for C string and G string (Swan)
FRANK BRIDGE. Allegro Appassionato (Stainer & Bell); *Pensiero* (Stainer & Bell)
B. J. DALE. Suite (Novello); *Phantasy* (Schott)
CYRIL SCOTT. Fantasia (Schott)
LIONEL TERTIS. *The Blackbirds* (Galliard); *Hier au Soir* (Schott); *Romance* (Schott); *Sunset* (Chester); *Tune* (Galliard); *Variations on a Theme of Handel*, for unaccompanied viola and cello (Francis, Day & Hunter)

---

* Many of the editions listed are now out of print. Some Galliard editions were originally published by Augener. All Murdoch publications were taken over by Chappell during the Second World War.

Arrangements of orchestral works

BACH. Double concerto in D minor for two violins, arr. for violin and viola (Boosey & Hawkes)

FREDERICK DELIUS. Double concerto for violin and cello, arr. for violin and viola (Galliard)

EDWARD ELGAR. Cello concerto (Novello)

HAYDN. Cello concerto in D, with a cadenza by L.T. (Boosey & Hawkes)

MOZART. Clarinet concerto (Chester)

Arrangements for viola and piano (except where otherwise stated)

ANON. *Fifteenth-Century Folk Song*, arr. for viola, cello and piano (Bosworth)

BACH. Adagio from the 'Great' Toccata and Fugue in C for organ (Boosey & Hawkes); Chaconne from Suite in D minor for unaccompanied violin, trans. to G minor (a fifth lower) for unaccompanied viola (Galliard); *Come Sweet Death*, from Schemelligesangbuch No. 42 (Schott)

BEETHOVEN. Cello sonata in G minor, Op. 5, No. 2 (Galliard); Minuet (Schott); Trio for two oboes and cor anglais, Op. 87, arr. for three violas (Bosworth); *Variations on a Theme from 'The Magic Flute'* (Boosey & Hawkes)

BRAHMS. Cello sonata in E minor, Op. 38 (Galliard); Clarinet sonatas Nos 1 and 2, Op. 120 (Galliard); *Wir wandelten* (song) (Boosey & Hawkes)

FREDERICK DELIUS. Caprice for cello and piano (Boosey & Hawkes); Elegy for cello and piano (Boosey & Hawkes); Serenade from *Hassan* (Universal); Violin sonatas Nos 2 and 3 (Galliard)

JOHN DOWLAND. *Elizabethan Melody*, arr. for unaccompanied viola and cello (Bosworth)

GALUPPI. *Aria Amorosa* (Galliard)

HANDEL. Arietta (Schott); Sarabande (Schott); Sonata in F (Boosey & Hawkes)

HAYDN. Capriccio (Schott); Minuet (Schott)

JOHN IRELAND. Cello sonata (Galliard); Violin sonata No. 2 in A minor (Galliard)

LISZT. *Liebestraum* (Galliard)

MÉHUL. Gavotte (Schott)

MENDELSSOHN. *Song Without Words*, Op. 19 (Schott)

MOZART. Clarinet concerto (Chester); Minuet (Schott)

PIERNÉ. Serenade, Op. 7 (J. Williams)

PORPORA. Aria in E major (Carisch)

REBIKOFF. Waltz from *The Christmas Tree* (Chester)

SAINT-SAËNS. Melody in B flat (Schirmer)

SCHUBERT. Allegretto in G, also arr. for two violas (or violins) and piano (Boosey & Hawkes)
SCHUMANN. Romance in F, Op. 28, No. 2 (Galliard)
CYRIL SCOTT. *Cherry Ripe* (Schott); *Fantasy* (Schott)
ETHEL SMYTH. *Two French Folk Melodies* (Oxford University Press)
SULZER. Sarabande (Schott)
SZYMANOWSKI. *Chant de Roxane* (Universal)
SEVCIK. *Violin Studies*, arr. for solo viola (Bosworth)
TRAD. *Irish Air* (Schott); *Londonderry Air* (Schott)
WILLIAM WOLSTENHOLME. Allegretto (Novello); *The Answer* (Novello); *Canzona* (Novello)

UNPUBLISHED WORKS

Works written for viola and orchestra
ARTHUR BENJAMIN. *Romantic Fantasy* for violin, viola and orchestra
YORK BOWEN. Concerto (*Phantasy* for viola and orchestra)
ADAM CARSE. Concerto
B. J. DALE. Romance and Finale, with cadenza by L.T.
J. B. McEWEN. Concerto
R. W. WALTHEW. *Mozaic in Ten Pieces*
WALDO WARNER. Suite in D, for viola and string orchestra

Works written for viola in small ensembles

W. H. BELL. Sonata for viola and piano
YORK BOWEN. *Fantasie* for four violas; *Romance* for viola and organ; *Romantic Poem* for viola, harp and organ
FRANK BRIDGE. Duet for violas
B. J. DALE. Introduction and Andante for six violas
HARRY FARJEON. Two pieces
KENNETH HARDING. Divertimento for four violas; Concertante for five violas
JOSEPH HOLBROOKE. Nocturne for viola, oboe d'amore and piano
LIONEL TERTIS. Obbligato to two songs by Brahms, Op. 91: *Longing at Rest* and *Cradle Song of the Virgin*; obbligato to song by Duparc: *Phidylé*; *Passacaglia on a Theme of Handel* for two violas or violin and viola; *The River*, for viola or soprano (words by L.T.) and piano
ERNEST WALKER. Sonata for viola and piano
RALPH VAUGHAN WILLIAMS. Romance for viola and piano (ed. Bernard Shore)

Arrangements for viola and piano (except where otherwise stated)
BACH. Double concerto in C minor for two violins, arr. for violin and

viola; Suite No. 3 for unaccompanied cello, arr. for unaccompanied viola

BRAHMS. *Minnelied*

CARTIER-KREISLER. *La Chasse*

DEBUSSY. *Minstrels*

JOHN DOWLAND. Duet arr. for soprano and viola

HENRY ECCLES. Cello sonata in G minor

CÉSAR FRANCK. Violin sonata

GLAZOUNOV. *Mélodie*

GRIEG. Song *I Love Thee*, arr. for viola; violin sonata in C minor, Op. 45, trans., arr. and ed. for viola in F minor

JOHN IRELAND. *The Holy Boy*

KALNINS. *Elégie*

MARIN MARAIS. Rondo in G

PADRE MARTINI. Violin sonatas in D and E

MENDELSSOHN. *Spring Song*

MOZART. Andante for two violas, from Duet in B flat for violin and viola; violin sonata in A; obbligato to aria from *Il Re Pastore*

RACHMANINOFF. Andante and Scherzo from cello sonata, Op. 19

REBIKOFF. *Berceuse* in A; *Dance of Satan's Daughter; Les Rêves; Insouciance*

GUY ROPARTZ. Cello sonata

ANTON RUBINSTEIN. Melody in F

SCRIABIN-KOCHANSKI. Etude No. 4

SULZER. Air on the G string

TCHAIKOVSKY. *Chanson Triste; Chant sans Paroles*

TURINA. *Farruca*

Recordings by Lionel Tertis

Discography compiled by Malcolm Walker

Vocalion Recordings, 1920–25*

BACH (arr. Tertis). Air on the G string/DALE:† with Frank St Leger (piano) – D-02067

BIZET (arr. Tertis). *L'Arlésienne* – Suite No. 1–3. Adagietto/SCHUMANN – R-6146

BRAHMS. Sonata in F minor for viola and piano, Op. 120/1 – 1st movement – X-9463 (03524/5); 2nd movement – X-9464 (03526/7); 3rd movement – K-05117 (03528/9)

CARTIER (arr. Kreisler). *La Chasse*/RUBINSTEIN: with Frank St Leger (piano) – R-6007 (1/21)

COUPERIN. *La Précieuse*: with anon. piano – R-6019 (4/21)

B. J. DALE. Suite for viola and piano – Romance/BACH: with Frank St Leger (piano) – D-02067, single-sided version A-0114

D'AMBROSIO (arr. Tertis). *Petite Suite* No. 2/KREISLER – R-6099

T. F. DUNHILL. Phantasy Trio in E flat, Op. 36; with Albert Sammons (violin) and Frank St Leger (piano) – R-6027

DUPARC. *Extase*: with Zoia Rosovsky (soprano) and anon. piano – L-5015 (2/22)

DVOŘÁK (arr. Tertis). *Bagatellen*, Op. 47: with Albert Sammons (violin) and Ethel Hobday (piano) – 1. Allegretto scherzando, 5. Poco Adagio – D-02083 (12/22) (02759 and 02762); 2. Tempo di Minuetto, 3. Allegretto scherzando – D-02111 (11/23)

FAURÉ. *Après un rêve*/COUPERIN: with anon. piano – R-6019 (4/21)

FAURÉ. *Elégie*/IRELAND: with Ethel Hobday (piano) – K-05144 (02592)

FUCHS. Duet/HANDEL (arr. Halvorsen): with Albert Sammons (violin) – D-02019

GODARD. Six duettini for violin and viola, Op. 18: with Albert Sammons (violin) and F. B. Kiddle (piano) – No. 1 – *Souvenir de Champagne*, No. 5 – *Minuit* – R-6063 (12/21)

---

* Coupling numbers given where known, followed by month and year of release (in brackets) and/or matrix numbers (also in brackets). Some records here listed are of extended duration.

† See separate entries for details of couplings.

175

GODARD (arr. Tertis). *Berceuse de Jocelyn*/MCEWEN: with Frank St Leger (piano) – D-02006

GRIEG (arr. Tertis). Violin sonata No. 3 in C minor, Op. 45 (arr. viola): with Ethel Hobday (piano) – D-02104/6 (9 and 10/23)

GRIEG (arr. Tertis). *I Love Thee*/MENDELSSOHN: with Ethel Hobday (piano) – R-6096 (02757)

HANDEL (arr. Tertis). Sonata No. 8, with Albert Sammons (violin) and F. B. Kiddle (piano) – 1st movement: Andante, 4th movement: Allegro – D-02033

HANDEL (arr. Halvorsen). Passacaglia/FUCHS: with Albert Sammons (violin) – D-02019 (4/21)

IRELAND. *The Holy Boy* (unaccompanied)/FAURÉ – K-05144 (03300)

KALNINS. (arr. Tertis). *Elégie*/SCHUBERT: with Ethel Hobday (piano) – D-02082

KREISLER. Rondo/D'AMBROSIO – R-6099

KREISLER. *Tambourin chinois* – Prelude and Allegro, after Pugnani: with Frank St Leger (piano) – D-02067

LISZT (arr. Tertis). *Liebestraum* No. 3/TERTIS: with Ethel Hobday (piano) – D-02144

MARAIS. *Le Basque*/MENDELSSOHN, SAINT-SAËNS: with anon. piano – R-6085

J. B. MCEWEN. *Breath o' June*/GODARD: with Frank St Leger (piano) – D-02006

MENDELSSOHN (arr. Tertis): *Songs without Words – Spring Song*/MARAIS, SAINT-SAËNS: with anon. piano – R-6085

MENDELSSOHN (arr. Tertis). *Songs without Words* – No. 1, Op. 19/1; No. 20, Op. 53/2: with Ethel Hobday (piano) – R-6115

MENDELSSOHN (arr. Tertis). *On Wings of Song*/GRIEG: with Ethel Hobday (piano) – R-6096 (02758)

MOZART. Trio in E major, K. 542: with Albert Sammons (violin) and Ethel Hobday (piano) – 1st movement: Allegro – D-02064 (9/21) (02539); 2nd movement: Andante grazioso; 3rd movement: Allegro – D-02091

MOZART. Trio in E flat: with Albert Sammons (violin) and Frank St Leger (piano) – 1st movement: Andante – D-02064 (9/21) (01782); 2nd movement: Menuetto, 3rd movement: Rondo – D-02015

MOZART (arr. Tertis). Trio No. 7, Op. 16: with Albert Sammons (violin) and Ethel Hobday (piano) – 1st movement: Allegro, 2nd movement: Andante – D-02150 (03301 and 03302); 3rd movement: Allegretto – K-05174 (03303)

RUBINSTEIN (arr. Tertis). Melody in F/CARTIER: with Frank St Leger (piano) – R-6007 (1/21)

SAINT-SAËNS. *Berceuse*/MENDELSSOHN, MARAIS; with anon. piano – R-6085

SCHUBERT (arr. Tertis). Trio in B flat, Op. 99/D898: with Albert Sammons (violin) and Ethel Hobday (piano) – 1st movement: Allegro moderato, 2nd movement: Andante un poco mosso – D-02050 (3/22); 3rd movement: Scherzo (Allegro), 4th movement: Rondo (Allegro vivace) – D-02060 (5/22)

SCHUBERT (arr. Tertis). *Ave Maria*/KALNINS; with Ethel Hobday (piano) – D-02082

SCHUMANN (arr. Tertis). *Slumber Song*/BIZET: with Ethel Hobday (piano) – R-6146

TCHAIKOVSKY (arr. Tertis). *Chanson Triste*; *Romance Sans Paroles*: with anon. piano – R-6017 (3/21)

TCHAIKOVSKY (arr. Tertis). *Barcarolle*/MOZART: with Ethel Hobday (piano) – K-05174 (02593)

TERTIS. *Reverie*/LISZT: with Ethel Hobday (piano) – D-02144

TRAD. (arr. Tertis). *Londonderry Air*/WOLSTENHOLME: with Frank St Leger (piano) – D-02011

WOLSTENHOLME (arr. Tertis). Allegretto/TRAD.: with Frank St Leger (piano) – D-02011

WOLSTENHOLME (arr. Tertis). *The Question*; *The Answer*; with Frank St Leger (piano) – D-02012 (11/23)

Columbia Recordings, 1925-33*

1925
BACH (arr. Tertis). Partita No. 2 in D minor, BWV1004 – Chaconne – L1644/5 (AX755, AX756, AX757, AX758)

BACH (arr. Tertis). *Come Sweet Death (Komm' Süsser Tod)* from *Schemelligesangbuch* No. 42: with Malcolm Sargent (pinao) – D1502 (A1468)

PORPORA (arr. Tertis). Aria: with anon. piano – D1502 (A1471)

WOLSTENHOLME. *Canzona* – D1569 (WA 4489–1, 2)

SCOTT. *Cherry Ripe* – D1569 (WA 4490–1, 2)

25 November
DOHNÁNYI (arr. Tertis). Sonata in C sharp minor, Op. 21: with William Murdoch (piano) – L1731/2 (WAX1160–1, 2, WAX1161–1, 2, WAX1162–1, 2, WAX1163–1, 2)

9 December
TRAD. (arr. Tertis). *An Old Irish Air* – L1761 (WAX1198–1, 2)
TERTIS. *Hier au Soir* – L1761 (WAX1199–1, 2)

1926
21 May
ARENSKY. *Berceuse*, Op. 30/2 – L1995 (WAX2191–1, 2)
KREISLER. Fugue in D after Tartini – L1995 (WAX1524–1, 2)

* Couplings here given in date order. Figures in brackets are matrix numbers.
13

KREISLER. *La Gitana* – D1554 (WA3282–1, 2)
SULZER. Air on the G string – D1554 (WA3286–1, 2)
SCHUBERT (arr. Tertis). *Du bist die Ruh'* – D1647 (WA5703–1, 2)
BACH (arr. Tertis). Adagio from C major Toccata, Adagio and Fugue, BWV364 – D1647 (WA5706–1, 2)
TERTIS. *Three Sketches* – i. *Serenade* – D1627 (WA5704–1, 2); ii. *Blackbirds* – D1627 (WA5702–1, 2); iii. *River* – D1628 (WA5707–1, 2)
TCHAIKOVSKY (arr. Tertis). *Chanson Triste* – D1628 (WA5705–1, 2)
GUIRAUD. *Mélodrame* – L2004 (WAX2192–1, 2)
DVOŘÁK (arr. Kreisler). *Slavonic Dance Theme No. 1* in G minor – L2004 (WAX1523–1, 2, 3)
SCHUBERT (arr. Tertis). *Nacht und Träume* – D1562 (WA3284–1, 2)
FAURÉ. *Après un Rêve* – D1562 (WA3285–1, 2)

28 November
BEETHOVEN. Trio in B flat, Op. 97 ('Archduke'): with Albert Sammons (violin) and William Murdoch (piano) – L1851–9 (WRAX2170–1, 2, 3, WRAX2172–1, 2, 3, WRAX2173–1, 2, 3, WRAX2174–1, 2, WRAX2175–1, 2, 3, WRAX2176–1, 2, 3, WRAX2177–1, 2, WRAX2178–1, 2, WRAX2179–1, 2, 3, 4)

1927
19 November
MOZART (arr. Tertis). Sonata in A major, K. 305 (arr. viola and piano) – Part 1 – L2070 (WAX3118–1, 2); Part 2 – Theme with variations – L2070 (WAX3119–1, 2)

BEETHOVEN (arr. Tertis). *Theme and Variations*, Op. 66: with Eric Gritton (piano) – Variations 2, 3, 4, 5 and 6 – L2172 (WAX3120–1, 2); Variations 7, 8, 10 and 12 – L2172 (WAX3121–1, 2)

HANDEL (arr. Tertis). Adagio non tanto – L2213 (WAX3122–1, 2); Allegro (WAX3123–1, 2) from Violin sonata, Op. 1/12 in F major

1928
19 June
RUBINSTEIN (arr. Tertis). Melody in F – 5230 (WA7513–1, 2)
TCHAIKOVSKY (arr. Tertis). *Chant Sans Paroles* – Op. 2/3 – 5230 (WA7514–1, 2)

BRAHMS. *Minnelied*, Op. 71/5 – D1637 (WA7517–1, 2)
MENDELSSOHN. *On Wings of Song* Op. 34/2 – D1637 (WA7515–1, 2)

TCHAIKOVSKY (arr. Tertis). *Chanson Triste* – DB396 (WA7518–1, 2)
TRAD. (arr. Tertis). *Londonderry Air* – DB396 (WA7516–1, 2) – all with Ethel Hobday (piano)

1929
25 March
MOZART. Trio in E major, K. 542: with Albert Sammons (violin) and
William Murdoch (piano) (unpublished) (WA8744-1, 2, WA8745-1,
2, 3, WA8746-1, 2, WA8747-1, 2, WA8748-1, 2, WA8749-1, 2, 3,
WA8750-1, 2, 3, WA8751-1, 2)

27 May
HANDEL (arr. Halvorsen). Harpsichord Suite No. 7 in G minor – Passacaglia: with Albert Sammons (violin) – L2364 (WAX4947-1, 2,
WAX4948-1, 2)
BAX. Sonata for viola and piano: with Sir Arnold Bax (piano) (unpublished) (WAX4949-1, 2, WAX4950-1, 2, WAX4951-1, 2, WAX4952-1,
2, WAX4953-1, 2, WAX4954-1, 2)

4 October
DELIUS (arr. Tertis). Violin Sonata No. 2: with Evlyn Howard-Jones
(piano) (unpublished) (WAX5190-1, 2, WAX5191-1, 2, 3,
WAX5192-1, 2, 3)

7 October
DELIUS (arr. Tertis). Violin Sonata No. 2: with George Reeves (piano) –
L2342/3 (WAX5193-1, 2, WAX5194-1, 2, WAX5195-1, 2, 3)
DELIUS (arr. Tertis). *Hassan – Serenade*: with George Reeves (piano) –
L2343 (WAX5196-1, 2)

1930
8 December
KREISLER. Prelude and Allegro after Pugnani – DX313 (WAX5906-1, 2)
LISZT (arr. Tertis). *Liebestraum* No. 3 in A flat – DX313 (WAX5907-1, 2)

TRAD. (arr. Tertis). *Londonderry Air* (unpublished) (WA10963-1, 2);
Lament (An Old Irish Air) (unpublished) (WA10959-1, 2)

MENDELSSOHN (arr. Tertis). *Songs Without Words* – Op. 19/1, *Sweet
Remembrance* – DB855 (WA10969-1, 2); Op. 53/2, *Fleecy Cloud*
DB855 (WA10964-1, 2): with Ethel Hobday (piano)

WOLSTENHOLME (arr. Tertis). Allegretto – DB1022 (WA10961-1, 2);
The Answer – DB1022 (WA10962-1, 2): with Ethel Hobday (piano)

1933
17 February
BRAHMS. Sonata in F minor for viola and piano, Op. 120/1: with Harriet
Cohen (piano) – LX225/7 (CAX6704-1, 2, CAX6705-1, 2, CAX6706-
1, 2, CAX6707-1, 2, CAX 6708-1, 2, CAX6709-1, 2)

30 April
MOZART. Sinfonia Concertante in E flat major for violin, viola and
orchestra, K. 364: with Albert Sammons (violin), London Philharmonic
Orchestra conducted by Sir Hamilton Harty – DX478/81 (CAX6824–1,
2, CAX6825–1, 2, 3, CAX6826–1, 2, 3, 4, CAX6827–1, 2, 3, 4,
CAX6828–1, 2, 3, 4, CAX6829–1, 2, CAX6830–1, 2, 3, CAX6831–1,
2, 3, 4)

26 October
TRAD. (arr. Tertis). *Old German Love Song*: with (orchestra) (unpublished)
(CA14102–1, 2)

MENDELSSOHN (arr. Tertis). *Venetian Gondola Song*, Op. 19/6: with
(orchestra) – DB1468 (CA14103–1, 2); *Song Without Words*, Op. 38/6 –
Duetto: with (orchestra) – DB1468 (CA14105–1, 2)

DVOŘÁK (arr. G. Walter). *Songs My Mother Taught Me*, Op. 55/4 –
with orchestra – DB1390 (CA14104–1)

H.M.V. Recordings
1947
BACH (arr. Tertis). *Come Sweet Death*: with anon. piano
SAMMARTINI. Sonatas, Op. 1, No. 2 in E major – allegro HMV C3619
(2EA12132–1, 2, 3)

LP reissue in 1966
MOZART. Sinfonia Concertante in E flat major for violin, viola and
orchestra, K. 364: with Albert Sammons (violin), London Philharmonic
Orchestra conducted by Sir Hamilton Harty
BRAHMS (arr. Tertis). *Minnelied*, Op. 71/5
MENDELSSOHN (arr. Tertis). *Songs Without Words* – No. 20 in E flat
LISZT (arr. Tertis). *Liebestraum* No. 3 in A flat
HANDEL (arr. Halvorsen). Harpsichord Suite No. 7 in G minor – Passa-
caglia with Albert Sammons (violin)
DELIUS (arr. Tertis). *Hassan – Serenade*
KREISLER. Prelude and Allegro in the style of Pugnani

HMV HQM1055

Since this Discography was compiled, it has come to light that recordings
of the following were made by Vocalion: MENDELSSOHN. Trio in D
minor, Op. 49: with Warwick Evans (cello) and Ethel Hobday (piano);
Trio in C minor, Op. 66: with Albert Sammons (violin) and Ethel
Hobday (piano); SCHUMANN. *Abendlied*/GRAINGER. *Molly on the Shore*;
COUPERIN. *Chanson Louis XIII* and *Pavane*/D'AMBROSIO. *Reverie*;
TERTIS. *Sunset*/REBIKOFF. *Les Rêves*; KERNGOLD. *A Piece*

Index